Dance Like a
Wave of the Sea

David Olio, Jr.

ISBN: 979-8-9920945-3-4

Cover design by: Betsy Petersen
Library of Congress Control Number: 2025902105
Printed in the United States of America

DEDICATION

To Steven, a student of the world~

CONTENTS

ACKNOWLEDGMENTS

Writing is a gift. It puts people in touch with others. It's true that writers can and do work in isolation, but they are never alone on the page. In this way, my former students were always present.

More, the writing process for me is interpersonal. A friend, Martha, had invited me into her writing world a year ago, when I had been stuck in an awful writing rut. Her writing world re-invigorate mine, and it would spur me back into my work, again, after many drafts.

Then, I received loving feedback from her, Nancy, and Teresa, in a reader group we built together. They read and discussed a *new* draft. I could only listen, which was the agreement. I gleaned a lot: first, *this* draft was working; second it needed more work.

Hearing feedback, though, rarely results in the thorough and deeply revised work a writer expects and needs to produce. As a result, Scott, a former colleague of mine at UConn, engaged me in conversation about the very purpose of my work, pushing me to say more, do more, and be more. He brought a wide lens and rich experience with literature, history, writing, and culture that helped me think more carefully. He was the writer's friend I needed. He's always been that guy.

Yet, I had needed strength, and my colleague and dear Low Rider friend, Shine, from Vermont, hardened my courage during the early days of a debacle I never anticipated. He helped steady my ship, sharing in the outrage and remaining strong when, well, I wasn't. I'm a lover, not a fighter; my Rider friend is both. That support ten years ago made this book possible.

In short, I admire those have who read, questioned, pushed, celebrated, supported and engaged with me in the love of ideas, writing, teaching, learning, and public engagement in honest inquiry into my life events in this memoir. I'm grateful for you all.

Mostly, I acknowledge the undying love of my best friend and partner, whose unwavering support for "that guy writing in the basement" allowed me time to write. She's wrapped her emotional-support-and-persistent arms around me and has not let go. She's even been my proofreader, along with two other loves of my life, David and Cassidy. (I'm responsible, though, for any typos folks find. And, I'm sure readers will find 'em! One has to give one's self some grace after respecting the written word with hours of one's time, though, when self-publishing.) Je t'aime, Teresa Marie. I love ya, too, my amazing kids.

The Fiddler of Dooney

When I play on my fiddle in Dooney
Folk dance like a wave of the sea
My cousin is priest in Kilvarnet
My brother in Moharabuiee

I passed my brother and cousin:
They read in their books of prayer;
I read in my book of songs
I bought at the Sligo fair.

When we come at the end of time,
To Peter sitting in state,
He will smile on the three old spirits,
But call me first through the gate;

For the good are always the merry,
Save by an evil chance,
And the merry love the fiddle
And the merry love to dance:

And when the folk there spy me,
They will all come up to me,
With 'Here is the fiddler of Dooney!'
And dance like a wave of the sea.

                                W B Yeats

1 SALUTATIONS

My Dear Students of 2015,

It's been ten years since I spoke to you all. I haven't spoken to you since being severed as your English teacher in February of 2015. It's hard to believe I'm finally writing to you. I've been trying to figure out exactly how to talk with you given that insane time. It's been nearly impossible to do, so I'm sorry this letter has taken so long.

I'd love to know that you are well. I'm sure you've been busy. Busy living your lives during a tumultuous American decade. You must have had a hell of a time, though, when your English teacher, who greeted you each day as you walked through the door of room 147, just vanished. I can't even imagine. Can't imagine what was going through your minds, sitting in our classroom in the days and weeks following, with the swirling rumors. Confusion over what had even happened. And for that, I'm sorry. I felt helpless. Forces came down on me from places I never imagined. My personal and professional worlds were torn apart. That's part of why it's been so hard to write you. I thought the whole affair would work itself out, and we'd be back exploring the world as readers and writers. But that didn't happen, and I've thought about you since.

I'm sure you remember the spectacle. It seemed our world lost its senses after a poem fell into the lap of my senior Advanced Placement Literature/University of Connecticut Early College Experience First-Year Writing course—quite a title! You remember, it was a poem that would draw the attention of the school, town, and nation. It certainly drew the

1

attention of the superintendent, who decided to put me on leave the next day. Then in two days following, the school system sought to fire me for discussing Allen Ginsberg's poem with that class. That just wasn't right. It felt cruel.

You likely remember some of that fateful day on February 25, 2015. I do. In my nineteenth year as an English teacher at South Windsor High School in Connecticut, I was working with eighty-six of you that second semester, also teaching other courses including four American Literature sections. In the AP/ECE class, twenty of you heard Allen Ginsberg read his poem "Please Master" on YouTube in the last twelve minutes of Period 2, that Tuesday. Those of you in the AP/ECE course were finishing poet presentations in a poetry unit titled "Voices in the Wilderness," when a student who had been inspired by an earlier presentation brought a book of Ginsberg's poetry off a bookshelf from home into class. He had questions about Ginsberg's language. He had also been working to narrow his senior thesis on "taboo" ideas, so he carried with him even more questions. At the time, I felt the class could handle a reading of this graphic poem in a teachable moment to conclude our inquiry into poets' use of language. We watched and listened to Ginsberg's own reading. We talked about questions such as whether the gritty, graphic language stood as gratuitous. Was it necessary for the narrator? Did the language effectively suit the poet's purpose? Was the poet's style effective? Why or why not? What was he getting at? Well, as you likely remember, instead of these questions floating around the school, the poem's language of a sexual act seeped into the school among students via text messages—it went viral, and not for the reasons of the work of our classroom.

The day after the class, two parents complained to the

school. I was pulled from my classroom and interviewed by the assistant superintendent and high school principal for twenty minutes. Then, dispossessed from my room keys and school badge, I was forbidden by the assistant superintendent from returning until further notice. I was not legally allowed to contact you. I would hear two days later in a letter from the superintendent's office that proceedings to fire me had begun. In the meantime, a tempest blew in the news and on Facebook. In those two days, a local news crew showed up to the school and interviewed a student who said he was in the class but was not. An anonymous parent was also quoted, commenting on the class without clearly knowing what had happened. The parent admitted as much. CNN reported on the reading. A gossip storm brewed.

So, I remained on leave, not allowed to contact you or step foot near the school. Isolated.

In the following weeks, despite the support of a flood of letters from current students, former students, parents of former students, and colleagues, the superintendent remained publicly silent. However, former students, residents, a parent of a student in the AP/ECE class, and my pastor along with twelve members from my church spoke at a Board of Education meeting. Their recollections of my past nineteen years of teaching failed to move the superintendent. I requested to talk with the two parents who expressed deep concern. Request denied. Silence reigned.

However, the superintendent did release a district-produced investigative report the assistant superintendent had scratched out and the subsequent termination letter to the local papers. Unbelievably, the superintendent warned I had been reported to police, and further I had been reported to the Department of Children and Families Services for Neglect and Abuse. Neither agency determined cause. That absolution couldn't even prompt discussion. Just some thinly veiled threats and vulgar remarks on social media sites remained. Fueled by gendered bias, some raged with bias, misinformation, and a lack of context. Mostly, though, silence about the class. I have a sense for what you must have been thinking and feeling, just not how you were processing this confusion. Some of you wrote me with tender words. I cried. I was not legally allowed to respond.

Well, you remember. The district would not relent. They claimed that allowing a poem in a senior class with multiple students seventeen years of age, under eighteen, should not have heard the poem, even though my lawyer noted a Harvard professor had written to the district, arguing the student's inquiry and return to class with the book was the highest act of scholarship: bringing inspired questions to a conversation for examination. Sure, it was not a poem that would be designed into an English curriculum taught on a high school campus, but it was brought in out of curiosity to senior class sanctioned by College Board and The University of Connecticut. Nevertheless, the impasse resulted in a necessary negotiation of my separation from the district. I was forced out of South Windsor Public Schools. And you were left without the English teacher you began the year with. And we haven't spoken since. I've stayed in touch with a group of students from that class and several families. Mostly, though: silence.

I've missed each of you since that day.

After it was all over, I tried to write about it all. After two terrible months ended, I wanted to re-fill the air at least with talk about reading, and writing, and learning. We needed to talk about what happened. There's so much left unsaid.

Unexamined.

I admit. I wanted to stand strong as your English teacher. I wanted to shield the voices of poets and writers who speak to us about the fullness of our full lives that I believed we're not just ignored but outright rejected. I wanted to advocate for those LGBTQ+ community members caught up in the ugly bias of reaction to the language of the poem. I wanted to stand for the community of participation where we would talk to each other with curiosity and respect. I wanted to defend your freedom to read and ask questions, practice democratic principles.

But the months rolled past, and I had not been able. Words were not working for me. School officials' words effectively silenced the work of our classroom. I remain haunted by the use of words to shut down conversation about learning, silencing exploration of the human experience. Those silencing words fueled by gendered bias, misinformation, and a lack of context. But I hadn't been able to marshal them. Turns out, though, they were working. Percolating beneath the surface. It's just taken some time. Revision. Trust. Persistence. So, in this letter, I assemble my words for you. They are me. You might call this letter to you a memoir. I'm not sure. I lived the life of an English teacher for thirty years and have been on this planet for sixty, and I'm still not sure about a lot. But I am sure this letter to you lives because of the power of writing. I possess a deep optimism in the freedom of inquiry empowered by words—and that will have to be enough—for now—in the face of forces that ignored the integrity of inquiry that I love. I believe so strongly in writing as ongoing dialogue that carries our exploration of life that it compels this letter to you. Conversation's the stuff of writing. It's the stuff of learning.

And, during this voyage on words, I hope we see it's also the stuff of democracy.

So, now I share this letter to you, in 2025, ten years later, and I hope my words ride on a current and dance with you like waves of the sea.

2 EARLY WORDS OF JOY

When I was five, living in the woods of Sherborn, MA, I fell in love with the world. Because there's so much to the woods and beyond, my life since has been a long series of dances with it all. If this really is a memoir, and I lean into past experiences that shaped my teaching with you, I first return to the woods. I translate those moments, though, not simply remember them. Writing offers me this moment now to settle down, quiet my mind, and re-shape words into new sentences. Revise and make sense of a complex past. Now. A new set of words organized to offer a fresh way of seeing. In my own translated story of a learner, looking back on my second-grade self in the woods along open fields in Sherborn, I have an impression of sheer delight.

No matter I was in the back yard in Sherborn, Massachusetts, in the early '70's, wandering the woods with my next-door neighbor, nibbling all day on the wild blackberries, blueberries and raspberries that dotted the bushes in the woods behind our houses, or whether I was in a classroom, exploring new and foreign fields planted itself into my being. I have always loved to learn. The world is a place of sheer fascination, and in Sherborn, as a physical, young boy, I loved to get out after it.

I remember walking along the horse path, which ran behind our house and that galloped for miles along the huge power lines off in the distance behind our house. I remember finding a pink Lady Slipper aside the path poking out from the forest floor. I also remember seeing just a few of these plants.

I had come across them from time to time, but they were not by any means widely found. Their reddish-pink veins seemed to hold a drooping pouch, and just one or two leaves extended from the stem. I also remember picking one to bring back to my mom, who quickly told me thanks but no thanks. The Lady Slipper was an endangered species, and they could live for up to twenty years—if some small boy didn't pick one for his mom—so we should not pick them but appreciate them in the woods. Learn to appreciate them. So, I did.

The lesson I learned that day taught me to look at the flora in the woods that were my playground as beautiful experiments, to watch them grow. I would crouch down, close to the loamy earth, with knees bent and eyes focused, and look. I would notice the low-growing pine surrounding these solitary flowers, which seemed to pop out of the ground every three or four inches. I later learned these waves of Princess Pine, sometimes growing out of large mats of moss and sometimes, which emerged out of the leaves themselves, cascaded for acres. I would later learn that these mini pines grew on a connected root system, and if you picked a piece or chunk of one, you could kill an entire area. Each plant, each with its own physical characteristics, is important to the network of roots. Words are like these networks, and my story lives only in the fibers of visibility. I need to uncover the complexity of that network under the ground of experience. It's writing's superpower. It's my hope that I can at least introduce the idea of exploration here in this letter to you, so we can acknowledge the interconnected network we all share, using this biological metaphor. So, we'll tread thoughtfully and with empathy in my letter to you. Writing is a process that allows us to uncover and then re-assemble, and I'm aware that many of you will reassemble this story in your own way, through your own lens.

I hope you are still writing. We understand people more, if we can find ways to take reflective tones. Clearly, you are likely writing more than any generation previous, having your noses buried in texts, email, social media posts, websites or blogs and—hopefully—writing some nonfiction, and even fiction, whether journaling, song writing, or perhaps even writing a poem here and there. Reflective writing, which is not strictly informative, like emails scheduling a meeting or a text that organizes a weekend away, seeks to make visible that which was not initially, and grow from it. This is where I hope to live in my letter to you. I hope to uncover the networks of influence upon our class on February 25th, 2015, and the days, weeks, and months that followed. One of the powers of language is to see anew and understand more. I hope to harness the power of language to acknowledge what had not been known, examine it, and begin to make sense of it outside of the common, running thought. It's what loving writers do. For sure, there has been too much silencing that ignored our experience. That silence threatens us all today. There are no mincing words with you here: silence diseases learning, and the disease is difficult to diagnose and even more difficult to treat.

Thankfully, when we are in conversation with writers and with others as a result, dialogue prompts us to rethink. Thoreau went to the woods to live deliberately. I went there in my early years and found joy in open exploration, back as a kid in Sherborn. For sure, the boundaries of the horse trail, the walls of a school, or other forms or resignation are important; and they frequently appear around us as learners. They take different forms for all of us. Some boundaries, though, are common. And the joy that drives us, the desire to know; the push to engage with the world regularly can trip us into falling face first into the ruts of conformity. We were caught in the tracks of censorship in 2015. It was one of the rips in the roots' network. And, at the time, we were pulled up like ugly weeds. Instead of discovery meant to destroy, it's for new growth. Joy's words about our learning we did together lay hidden and unspoken, until now. Here. On this page. As Langston Hughes wrote, in "Theme for English B,"

> It's not easy to know what is true for you or me
> at twenty-two, my age. But I guess I'm what
> I feel and see and hear, Harlem, I hear you:
> hear you, hear me—we two—you, me, talk on this page.

I'm so glad we're all finally talking about the joy of learning in us all.

I turn my eye, just down the road from my back woods to a story my mother has told me about my wide-eyed joy as a little learner in a classroom image at Pine Hill Elementary, Sherborn, MA—a fuzzy impression. It comes as if I were looking back through dirty old binoculars, wrapped in cracked leather. The ugly grime of my personal experience with the South Windsor district after that February day in 2015, clouded my view of a classroom, but I have the choice to clean the lenses. So, I can now see through the elementary school window, into the room. I sweep the room, zooming in on rows of old desks with open cubbies underneath for books, lined yellow paper, construction paper, and colored pencils with pencil sharpeners; my memory lens pans across the teacher's large wooden desk, with her sitting behind it and a blackboard behind her. This image would not now exist, though, without the words I choose now to make this image visible. It's a calling forth a word frame in new time.

Over the long sections of blackboard, I see a set of scripted ABC's unfurl, with each letter elegantly written. That's all, really. Just the letters to memorize. Now, they are bright yellow against chalk-board green. The capital letter "A" dances in curved moves. Now, it transforms itself into a lower-case "a," still as vibrant, even sassier in its smaller serif, ready to go as a single letter. A phoneme. An article. Or, part of the longer word "article." Language offers so many options. It rarely, if ever, means just one thing. I remember and transform the image. Mixed feelings dangle from the image-memory with mixed letters. I sense the urge of a raised hand. I remember the frustration of an arm waving and waving and waning. Waiting and waiting. However, now, there's much more. Always so much more that writing helps discover.

My mother has told it as a love story. Complete love. In her words, I loved school. She has told me I was that little, rapt boy who fidgeted mightily behind a little desk, mesmerized by the teacher and her speech. My mom has named me as that little boy sitting at the edge of his seat, chest pressed forward. I was that little boy with short, cropped hair in 1972, with right hand vaulting outward toward the teacher, with the little left hand, gripping beneath the right arm elbow, pushing the fleshy arm with its fingers extending from the hand out toward the teacher. I was that little boy who begged to answer a question—who had a thousand more questions. I would learn to put those letters to use, just as I write now.

My mom has spun her story of me not just a few times. She has knit her story with my enthusiasm. That giddiness was interminable, she told me, in my second-grade classroom. As I think back on it now, I am awash in gratitude for Mrs. Grey, who worked with at least twenty-five other 2nd graders. Led us through a parade a letters. Because she empowered the room's enthusiasm brought forth by each seven-year-old. She nurtured each imagination integral to the human experience. I now feel more appreciative and emboldened. Hers was a monumental responsibility. Public school teachers hold our intellectual, emotional, and social development in their imaginations. They need to allow us to explore, and I was one who was so excited by Mrs. Grey that I thrust my little hand in the air, poking it like my own needle coming up through the fabric, waiting to turn, head down, and then thrust back up. As I tell the story, though, I would not get that opportunity as much as I would have liked in school, which would help shape my teaching philosophy. I believe in students activating their learning in connection with the world—with our mentors prompting it. Often, a classroom's learning limits eyes to staring at a desk—a chalkboard. Bland, made-up audiences remain within four walls, disconnected and only generally imagined, rather than pushing on direct, purposeful stakes. Learning offers us opportunities to explore our relationships with the world, and that exploration should be honest, authentic. It's a belief that has helped me find this hybrid letter/memoir form, to write to you.

I imagine you, too, have deeply fond memories of elementary school. Maybe ones associated with a drawing that hung on your refrigerator of your pet; maybe one is associated with a sound from the band room of your first note with your flute, puffing its way through that shiny, silver vessel; maybe one's the touch of a friend's hand as you went out to recess to run in the open air, flirting with friendship itself. I hope that joy had some outlet. I hope you can express some facet of it. I'm doing my best here on this page, with these words: to express my early joy in learning.

Teachers, like parents, are a product of their own experiences growing up. My mother shared pleasant acknowledgements of curiosity, along with the more devilish inventions of capturing imagined foes in chalk-drawn traps with stick-made weapons. Mrs. Grey passed along her observations though in both side conversations in town as well as school reports. Report cards, on their yellow card stock, with beautiful teacher handwriting numbering my performance, told of my enthusiasm for school. But, I find my mother's knitted story that has warmed me at night from the start: I have always loved to learn.

These early habits settled deeply within me, so as I look back now, I recall discovering those boundaries that can muffle and silence a healthy dialogue of learning. In this letter, I'm reminded discovery is neither easy nor without implications. I'd love to tell you in this letter that the joy of learning is all joy. Let's go back, further, though, before Sherborn, MA.

In 1964, a white child was born in Richmond Memorial Hospital in Richmond Virginia. He was born to what our American culture now calls white, middle-class parents, who were making their best effort to start a family. At that time, however, the term "white" generally lacked awareness in middle-class America. This child, then, like so many in America, would have to travel a path of learning to understand the social complexities of world he came into. This infant, like so many, would not know the conditions he was born into. No one whispered to him about them. White, middle-class voices lacked even the words of acknowledgement. Despite the good trouble of the sixties, most white kids like him, as they grew up, would be raised in a world of silence: class, racial, and gendered bias just rumbled on during the tumultuous era of American Civil Rights. Neary a word of great challenge to our burdensome problems of racial injustice would the boy hear. He would have to learn on his own as he grew older. He would have to read widely, speak to others outside of his community's limited language, and raise questions during his late adolescence and undergraduate life. He would have to grow while he married, have children. He'd have to take classes for his master's degree and deeply wrap his incredulous head around the world he had been reared in. When, eventually, he would become. A teacher.

My family's collection of black and white photos tells a story of a certain division: The lone small brick house I first lived in with a fenced back yard. The dog house in the rain. The empty swing on a third birthday party. In the birthday party picture, several small white boys sit at a picnic table in the back yard. Each has a crew cut. Each has a white t-shirt. Each with jeans rolled at the cuffs. Each with saddle-shoes with a brown swipe of leather. The mothers in the photo, each have short-bouffant cuts. Black-rimmed cat glasses. My mother is not wearing glasses. All smiling. Still all homogenous.

Unlike the Kodachrome cameras to eventually produce colored photos, these images sit in albums on matted paper, yellowed and aging, conveying a deceptive sense of black-and-white and order and stability...but division. No people of color in a city of colored people in the late 1960's. I believe conditions of bias have always existed, and so they did in Richmond, VA in 1964-1969, when I was born and first lived. As I write to you, I don't think back with confusion or judgement. I just wonder where the multiple pathways of thinking can come from? Which voices would remain quiet, outside of my experience? What are the effects of the singular perspective that lives on as *the* way to think?

It's crazy. I was born in Richmond Memorial Hospital just four miles from Jefferson Davis's house. As the President of the Confederacy, he first called Mississippi his home, having been born there and then having cast allegiance to follow its secession from the Union. He then lived in Richmond, Virginia, as President. The home of ultimate national division. Turns out, his house on 1201 E Clay Street was never mentioned to me during my life. Richmond Memorial Hospital, now Ginter Place, a renovated building for condominiums, had moved toward that infamous address in 1987, when the Richmond Memorial Foundation relocated its services. I generally knew about Jefferson Davis when I was much older, but I had no idea the house I first lived in was down the street from his former abode. The home of The Confederacy.

Turns out, as I discovered when assembling language for my letter to you, that Richmond Memorial Hospital was started in 1957 as a memorial to the men and women who died during World War II. According to the Foundation, "The Hospital opened its doors to people of all races and backgrounds, regardless of their ability to pay." I have been amazed to learn, too, it also played a key role as a provider of health care services during the baby boom of the late 1940's. My mother had been a registered nurse for a doctor who also worked in the hospital where I was born. I like writing you about this research, learning that Richmond Memorial was one of the first to admit certified black doctors into the hospital—first in Richmond. It's an important connection to me, as my life began in a community whose Monument

Avenue had been the home of huge memorials honoring confederate figures from the Civil War, such as Jefferson Davis, Stonewall Jackson, and Robert E Lee. The street is no longer lined with these memorials, as they were torn down or removed after the protests and public conversations following the murder of George Floyd in 2020. Now, only a statue of the great tennis player Arthur Ashe remains. As I write to you, I just cannot recall any conversation about these monuments within my family during my lifetime. Certainly not one conversation that acknowledged out loud the racism behind the establishment and maintenance of those memorial symbols of the Confederacy nor the changes the citizens of Richmond have so importantly wrought. So much hard work. Now, as I seek to make visible the forces surrounding the reaction to our reading of the Ginsberg poem, I write and juxtapose these images. And I breathe. I reflect on and reassemble with my words to you in this letter my humble beginnings.

I see bubbling. I'm sure you've had teachers who spoke difficult words about oppression and crafted lessons with a justice framework in mind. Many of my colleagues had recognized the growing shifts in America and applied and educational approach that sought to recognize and respect all identities of all students. Some, teachers, of course, tangled with and were more articulate and passionate in their work toward inclusion, such as my cooperating teacher and other colleague, whom I'll tell you more about later. But, I hope you still continue to do your own research—and reflect on and unpack the assumptions of your own experience. Write about it. Think about it. Ask questions. Dance with the multiple ways of viewing the world. In my formative days, people in my orbit did not acknowledge, much less reflect on, racial or gender bias. So it continued. I would have to learn that on my own as a reader. As a student. As an English teacher.

As I bring my early-found joy to you in this letter, I acknowledge a silenced story of my beginning, in Richmond, Virginia: my birthplace. I post a sign for you here about my joy of pick-axing the hard earth that covered not only the red clay geography of Richmond but also my early years in a segregated city. While I was born and raised under a happy façade of family, others' experiences of suffering discrimination remained ignored and silenced. Not all democratic voices—of ALL Richmond citizens—were allowed but remained buried beneath the louder frequency of the daily world, of jobs and dreams. The exclusion and the silencing effect of bias contradicts a carefully protected story of innocence, fairness, and opportunity for all. I believe many recognize this as American myth. The experiences of struggle to belong remain ignored. They only emerge into the public consciousness from time to time but are sadly beaten down with silence. So, I write to you about them. It's inspirational when words, music, paintings, sounds, dance and other forms of art have enlivened people's experiences and give them buoyancy. I believe the arts celebrate the capacity for human experience, countering the silences of the past and present. That's a joy. Odd, isn't it, that many acknowledge the value of the arts yet sometimes reject legitimacy of some in our communities? So, I pick ax. And there's joy in it. Finding. Learning.

It takes time, though. Just as it's been difficult to unearth that day when a student brought in his questions about a challenging poem about a gay sexual act. Did you know, for example, that schools were segregated in early 1964, my birth year? I hadn't, either when I lived there—and for a good deal of time after we moved. The conversation about segregation had not been part of my white American world. As I think about it, the past was tucked away like a banished criminal in the conversation following the reading of the Ginsberg poem in our class that so upset some people. We didn't have the chance to consider the forces of the past that inform our present. Maybe, if we had had a community-wide conversation, which we had begun in class, that included a consideration of the past's influence during the 1950's and 1960's and contextualized Ginsberg's oeuvre, we might have built a more productive conversation than relying on a claim of obscenity. Of listening to another's perspective. Of walking a mile in someone else's moccasins.

But as I write to you about early words of learning joy, I come across the amazing moments that did address social injustice but sit densely packed in that black hole of material trapped by the silence of tradition and bias. Legally speaking, the Brown v. The Board of Education of Topeka, Kansas ruling in 1954 unraveled almost 100 years of public-school legal segregation, including in Richmond. But, the dominant, white voice, who claimed and declared those who stood for justice as "agitators" would, of course, continue. Suffocating. You likely know the denial and the claims of white innocence that has routinely existed in the south and the north in relation to racism; in fact, a strong counter narrative has always existed where words like "inclusion," "critical race theory" and "racism" have been slashed at, torn up, and otherwise rejected. The bloodied words struggle to remain in the consciousness of enough people to break through the intended silence. So I write to you; I offer to open this conversation. I hope to bandage the damaged words of open discourse, suffered by bias's silencing. I hope this triage is not too late.

In 1964, the year of my birth, the Voting Rights Act was passed, after incredible events of violence designed to maintain the status quo in the south, Richmond, Virginia. Yet, rarely if ever in one's education during the '60's and '70's did teachers in white public education systemically address the problem of social injustice that plagued Richmond, Virginia, the former capital of the Confederacy, and all the other places throughout the country. In my letter, I can take time to add nuance here. Directly address you to say that educators have had words to describe injustice, if they wanted them, from their predecessors and writers. We should take the time to qualify my claim of ignorance. I can tell you that some teachers did acknowledge and address injustice. Jane Eliot is a well-known example, after the PBS Documentary *Blue Eyes/Brown Eyes Exercise* shared her lesson focused on empathizing with other's point of view, specifically the marginalized. This work, a discussion about the "other,"—of those pushed to the outer edges from our white, straight, communities—was unique, however. It seems I need now—in 2025—still defend the naming of racial and gender inequities that plagued my generation. So, I will not excuse my phrase "white, straight communities" in the United States: racial and gender inequality was built into my community like the Lincoln Logs I played with as a kid, piece by piece and fortressed into pretty much everyone. Moreover, as much as race and gender were beginning to become part of the national discussion, gay rights were not on the radar yet. The term LGBTQ+ would not emerge until the 2000's. Very little of this conversation had breath in white neighborhoods like mine. And it certainly was not mentioned in the schools I attended. So I write to you with the belief that the written word can identify the silence that bias wields, to open new conversation, and spur our democratic habits. We need words of conversation.

In 1964, when I was born, the country was yet again on the verge of this consciousness. We've had moments of collective consciousness. Justice had poked its nose around during Reconstruction but then was denied. Jim Crow laws kept black people from voting; from eating at white lunch counters; black musicians—those who did not pass as white— from sleeping in all-white motels; from education in all-white schools. Efforts to organize and get people to the polls, to enter a restaurant to eat where they wished, and to go to school with equal opportunities were met with clubs, guns, and white hoods. Later in the 1960's, consciousness bubbled, too. Bill Russell was making history in Boston with the Celtics in the NBA — which hadn't allowed black basketball players as habit — as arguably the greatest defensive basketball player ever. Instead white neighbors vandalized Russell's home, broke in, smeared the walls literally with shit. Consciousness is fleeting.

I write to you now, though, that discover connects us to other's experience. I trust in it for its motivation. I'm sure it drives me to the page, so I continue to write, seeking a way for us to talk. It's my personal form of persistence. This epistolary form allows my personal voice, and it's been a long time coming. I urge myself to work the words to move out of their hiding. My own discovery won't drown if I can write to you about learning.

Of course, there's more beneath the surface to dive into, and, as I grew and learned and discovered, I share with you that which remained silent in and about Richmond,

Virginia—the state where I was born in and lived my first six years. Miscegenation laws kept black and white people from marrying. I've been told, "No, marriage would not have happened" at that time, not necessarily because of laws but because collective habits of bias prevented it. Yes, the Virginia legislature finally eliminated the laws in 1967, when I was three years old, but the personal prejudice remained. How would I know looking back at those photos of my home of my family of the people in my neighborhood that laws existed to keep people of different races from marrying? How would I know the people around whom I lived harbored such low opinions of a group of people? One wouldn't know unless it was openly acknowledged. As we grow up and become socialized within our own communities, we see things around us, and we take those things as truth. It's not your doing that your parents, their neighbors, and their community members forward practices that they have not questioned as potentially unjust and demeaning to the human spirit. Culture works in way like this: our families, our institutions all carry messages about who is included and who is excluded. And it's very difficult to talk about that exclusion when it remains unacknowledged and buried in acceptance. We always seem to be able to talk about who's included; however, we rarely discuss exclusion.

When the famous US Supreme Court ruling of Loving v. Virginia, decided on June 12th, 1967, that Virginia's anti-miscegenation statutes violated the Constitution's 14th amendment and had to be changed, the decision effectively overturned all bans on interracial marriage in sixteen states. As I think back about the silence in my youth and the silence in my state, the silence of justice also remains as I sit down to write you this letter. In order to learn about Loving v. Virginia in this letter, I joyfully place words on the page to address difficult truths. In my birthplace and beyond, people's prejudices have hidden in institutions, including the law, afraid to acknowledge the human spirit in others. To delegitimize people of color as legitimate partners in a marriage breaks my heart. It's shocking, isn't it? But, we can celebrate here on this page. Now, in my letter to you, we can acknowledge out loud the legitimacy of marriage is available to people regardless of their skin color. Consciousness once again flickers.

This famous case would be cited forty years or so later in 2013 in Bostic v. Schaefer, which was a lawsuit filed in federal court that challenged Virginia's refusal to sanction same-sex marriages, period. Now I'm familiar—very familiar—with the long path in the United States not only for people of color but also people in the LGBTQ+ community who have had to scrape, scrap, and claw for their own legitimacy out of a seemingly silent block of cold and unyielding stone—a block of stone with no reverberating sound of their human warmth and truth. Just a cold no. A cold, continuing socialized set of habits and practices that have firmly held that they do not have human rights.

So, on July 18th, 2013, Tim Bostick and Tony London, two gay men who had lived in Norfolk, a town near my home city of Richmond, where other of my family had also lived at one time, filed the lawsuit that challenged the state's ban on same sex marriage. The District Court would come to rule the law unconstitutional, that there is a fundamental right. The decision cited Loving v. Virginia, which had been filed in the same District Court of Virginia. You may not know this about this case, but in two year's time, the Supreme Court of the United States ruled in Obergefell v. Hodges that same sex couples in the United States, no matter where they live, have the same legal right to marry as different sex couples.

You know, we're too often told that reflecting honestly on the past wastes time. Maybe so, if we simply repeat the same. Over and over. I believe writers re-animate learning with words. It takes time to dig them out of material of longstanding habits and ways of thinking. Our world's new every day when we take the time to acknowledge old tracks in the woods and make new ones. The page is a place of past reflections we can draw from. It's a place of possibility when we use words to reflect with intentions of exploration.

3 WORDS OF INQUIRY: HOW SO? ASK!

Can We Acknowledge and Ask Real Questions?

The second day after I was removed as your teacher, a wave of incrimination and calls for punishment began. The principal's office at the high school, the assistant superintendent of personnel's office, and the superintendent's office picked up the charge—even random people who didn't know me or the work of our classroom joined in. But my confidence in inquiry buoyed me, and for periods of time, the conversations I had with my family, my colleagues, a parent from the AP class, letters from then-current and then-former students, and my own trust to still engage with the world kept my nose above the waterline. I wonder how much direct thought people sink into the idea of inquiry, so I write to you in this letter about a confidence in inquiry in contrast to the singular idea of handling the reading of a poem with punishment.

I've started writing to you about joy and authentic learning—I wish it for each of you, in all you do. But it was impossible to move beyond the claims of criminality ten years ago, and it's still no small challenge now. A too oft repeated phrase can create a thinking-rut, so I'd like to lean on a new term when we put the joy of discovery front and center that was essentially ignored: "confidence in inquiry." I've always held that we can rely on sense of joy as an inherent characteristic of inquiry. This is not a confidence of blind hope in the success of inquiry but a deep belief in its process.

Confidence doesn't target a goal or certainty of accomplishment itself, but it exists for the sake of the discovery.

For sure, it can be hard for some to relate to a confidence when it comes to teachers. Confidence in inquiry can be misinterpreted as arrogance. Being cocky. However, nothing is farther from the truth. I mean, engaging in inquiry is a lot like geeking out. Like the phrase "geek out," confidence in inquiry signals engagement and appreciation for unyielding passion. That deep joy threatens some. It means letting down a guard or carefully held and protected façade of control. After all, who knows where you'll really land? Who knows where you end up if you're really open-minded and engaged in inquiry? I've learned over time that our habits are cable thick. So many layers of twisted threads hold together those habits—and strengthens the façade of control. A poem, for example, turned people's crystal to look at the world in a way that either they weren't used to or even disapproved. What had been a moment of potential inquiry into learning after that classroom in February 2015 was transformed into something entirely dirty after that day—twisted into some kind of crime. How did that happen? How did the silence take over? Why did the silencing happen? How did that silence emerge to suffocate all of us? I'm trying to make a writing move here to alert you to the notion that control and power inherently left no room for the idea and practice of inquiry. There lacked a confidence in inquiry. Instead, any perceived other way of thinking was deemed dangerous. A direction other than the status quo undermines power. Inquiry becomes a threat in and of itself. So, instead of seeing a student bringing his curiosity and questions to class as fundamentally valuable, a potentially open discussion instead turned to some form of punishment. We need a real confidence in inquiry, to fuel conversations about learning and teaching, else there's no air for the fire that's discovery.

I know, it's been a long time since we've talked about learning. I'd like to draw attention to conditions students have experienced and inhabited that drive the need for confidence of inquiry. I'd like to take you back to the 90's, not as a trip down nostalgia-of-teaching lane but as several experiences that can help us consider conditions that prompt real questions. In 1997, for example, anyone walking the halls of the South Windsor High School — or any high school in the country, for that matter — would likely hear a common phrase used to identify anything that was considered "bad." Students would say, "That's so gay." This language had become so common place it could be heard in daily conversation in the café, hallways, and classrooms. The phrase became so omnipresent the faculty needed to address it, so we did during a faculty meeting; we all agreed that it demeaned gay people in the exchange and fostered a threatening learning environment of all—these were words aligning LGBTQ+ people with unacceptability, and were essentially used to put other people, whom the speaker in some way did not like or did not approve, in their place. Students would launch the word "gay" and "faggot" as weapons of attack. We all felt the sting of that pejorative language, and cruel language towards others in an educational community drowns learning. A democratic tool has always been freedom of speech, so it's important to talk about responding to speech in healthy communities. I'm sure you're thinking now about weaponized language used today; and if you are, then the words of my heartfelt letter to you are having an additional impact to laying out the ignored, foundations of inquiry and learning inherent in the AP/ECE class that have remained silenced since February 25, 2015.

Well, some faculty tried to address the term with students. I remember starting a conversation with a student who'd just fired the phrase from a sling-shot in the English wing. Hanging out at my door during passing time to shoot the breeze with students and colleagues, I asked if they really thought about the term. In most cases, such as one I recall in the hallway, the student just wasn't aware of the implications. The demeaning consequences didn't resonate, but after a conversation, students usually see another point of view and reconsider their own. It took a long time, though, to continue those conversations with students, and I think they were effective in helping forge conditions of confidence, with respect for all, enjoining students in learning.

My mind leaps back to the first Human Relations Committee (HRC) meeting in the front office in 1996 as an example of the torn fabric of respect for all, which undermines students' ability to be active learners. The HRC initially began as a faculty study of the challenges facing the school community, as demographic populations accelerated in diversity. No longer was the town an all-white, agricultural rural community of the mid-1900's. I remember the ten-foot-long rectangle table in the front office meeting room, with seats for many, behind a full wall of windows—an open and inviting environment. Teachers crowded around the table at 6:30 am before school to discuss the school's climate and plan how to create conditions to nurture all students: it was a meeting of the HRC.

My colleague and former cooperating teacher had encouraged me to attend — I had just been hired in 1996 full-time. So, I joined. As I think back on her influence on me, I'm warmed. She helped me guide my energies, just as we do as teachers for our students. In fact, each individual needs to feel a sense of belonging within a community to practice their own emboldened ardor for learning, so I've always worked to respect each colleague and student as a capable human being, with special compassion toward individuals struggling to belong. We have all felt the pang of exclusion and the sting of marginalization. So, this specific work began in the HRC to address conditions that limited learning. My first year at South Windsor, after working at Cathedral High School, a parochial school in Springfield, Massachusetts for three years, allowed me to begin new commitments to add to a learning community.

The committee engaged in intense discussion over the very meaning of the word "diversity" and ways to support not only those who struggle with the deeply entrenched high school stereotypes but also those who contend with long-standing societal prejudice. After that first meeting, I learned more of the intense need to make room for students who become invisible as individuals to the people surrounding them in a socialized institution. The feeling of invisibility is debilitating. We've all experienced it. Ralph Ellison's narrator, Invisible Man, who suffered from deeply entrenched and layered stereotypes and assumptions, reminds us of the universal connection we all share to the eponymous novel, Invisible Man, when he asks us, "Who knows but on the lower frequencies I speak for you?" To make room is to connect with each other. I've since reflected that our connections with each other are pathways for inquiry, and I believe that environments must be constructed to foster crackling airways of collaboration.

After my first HRC meetings, I was emboldened as a

young educator to contribute to a school and to a profession that would focus on figuring out educational pathways to prepare students for authentic democratic citizenship. Unfortunately for the Human Relations Committee, the principal retired from South Windsor High School—and with him the committee went dark. As a result, planned, concrete actions waned, and attention wavered. The new administration's priorities shifted elsewhere, and the focus on problem-solving difficult climate problems affecting students decreased. Some don't like to hear the honest truths about the pain experienced when one's learning is interrupted or prevented. Examining the field for fair competition frequently exposes hierarchies of power. During that era, difficult conversations arose over the very need and effectiveness of community learning and problem-solving. Disagreements about even whether to address difficult issues shut down opportunities to honestly speak in public about the problems that faced students in high school. And, as you well know. There are many.

However, an English department colleague who had been my cooperating teacher in 1992 and I re-formed the group. This time we envisioned the group as comprised by students—and led by students. My colleague and I set out to train students as leaders in democratic problem-solving and conflict resolution. Because my colleague and early mentor and I deeply believed in the work, we volunteered our time to take that work head on. We wanted to open learning to all students, including those with diverse backgrounds. In our own classrooms, we created a smaller, after-school version of the Human Relations Committee with students as members and, most importantly, as leaders—we also invited faculty members. The students passionately dove into the work, as well; so, collaboratively, we served as advisors for the students and conducted the diversity training, bringing in experts in the field and discussing issues after school. All of us sought to scale the work through the student body. We spent countless hours prepping for these meetings and programs in room 147 and 149, packed with up to thirty students in a room designed for twenty, all giving our time and imaginations to conceiving a community where over 1,500 students, each unique and stellar within the varied dimensions of race, ethnicity, age, religion, gender identity, socioeconomic status, physical condition, intellectual condition, political belief, and ideology, could engage in community inquiry.

The Bead Activity

For example, the group trained students to reflect on their community relationships, to consider the ways we believe the socially-constructed idea of race plays in our lives. To facilitate this exploration, my co-advisor and I had researched and discovered the "Bead Activity." Given approximately fifteen categories, such as Next-Door Neighbor, Favorite Athlete, and Prominent Politician, etcetera, students would identify individuals in their lives and select a bead coordinated to a racial category. For instance, given the race of their dentist, their favorite musical artist, their best friend, an authority figure important to them, they would color-coordinate the beads. As a result, students would create a bead bracelet, selecting any order for their colored beads. They could then wear it on their wrists or put it on their backpacks—they could do with the bracelet what they wanted. However, the presentation teams comprising Human Relation Committee students put the activity in context by brainstorming the socially constructed definitions not only of diversity but also of race. Each visited an English class. Then, along with each respective class teacher, they facilitated a reflective activity to identify the combinations of race and ethnicities of people whom they associated with and those whom they encountered by chance in the community. This community-wide, powerful experience allowed them to reflect on a representation of relationships. The beads served as visual representation, empowering students to reflect on the degree of choice they felt they had in creating more racial and ethnically diverse relationships. It allowed them to discuss difficult choices or the absence of those choices that colored their lives. An integrity in pursuing questions allowed us to discover connections and gaps in our lives we would have never imagined otherwise. We discover truths important to the understanding of each other in our communities in ways that can empower us in democratic conversation and by acknowledging others' experience.

This work not only uncovered intense moments of pride, of course, but also deeply-seated prejudiced assumptions about the socially-constructed concept of race in our community. Some students wondered why we were talking about race. That problem had been solved, they said. Well, as we know, biases based on socially-constructed categories existed and still exist today. It's a feature of human nature that should be discussed and addressed to best support learning environments thriving in inquiry. Writing this letter to you has led me to this important point.

"We live in a 'color-blind' world," some white students participating in the Bead Activity claimed. Others rejected the idea that their beads even represented a fundamentally white set of relationships, which was ironic, given the racial demographics in South Windsor, still a majority white town. Some even angrily drew conclusions that the activity was rigged, saying that just because their barber or hairdresser, religious leader, teacher and best friend were all white that they were "not racist," when no one had even made that claim. Instead, beads do not inherently challenge but simply reveal a cultural pattern of relationships. These students struggled to understand the activity an inventory and reflection activity. And it's no surprise, as socialization works in this way: people are acculturated into ideas as truths for all rather than beliefs. More, folks who have been raised within privilege tend to ignore this and even reject it. After all, admitting privilege does acknowledge imbalance exists. Today, as I write you, many people reject this concept. I understand. People feel accused. But, when ignoring imbalance, we perpetuate it. People generally do not want to think of themselves as mean-spirited. Who does? Still, some others may want to maintain the inherent advantage. Keep the hierarchy that way. According to this thinking, the natural order has positioned us this way. They will say, "Well, that's the way it is and that's the way it has always been." (As far as they can see). In general, it seems a part of human nature to avoid conflict, especially if it involves one's own world view. I believe an education must include honest conversations where reflection allows a close inquiry into habits, values, and assumptions. This was some of the most moving stuff of discovery.

However, a much larger subset of students recognized the cultural influence and wondered about their own core values. What did they believe, actually? What did they believe about socialization? What did they believe about their role in developing relationships? Would they begin to break up the dominance of racialized relationships? For what reasons? We asked questions about the degree one should have varied racial relationships. They asked, why? What would be the benefit to the individual? To others of color? To those of the predominantly white community? To their community? To their country? They asked How? How might we open ourselves to new relationships? What assumptions would one need to reconsider? What habits might need to change? As we would discuss in our Human Relations Committee debriefing exercise afterwards, when people take a gem out of a box and hold up that idea to the light, twisting and turning and thinking, a level of honest and earnest conversation emerges. As a result of the Bead Activity, higher levels of questioning and of discord made for an authentic experience. It was a moving and effective activity, and we all were dancing like waves of the sea.

Students had guided careful thought and discussion with classmates—with their immediate school community. I remember a deep joy for the students as I checked in on each of the presenter groups while they ran this training for their own classmates. My English colleagues, who had graciously and thoughtfully agreed to offer their homeroom time for the presentations, were amazed not only by their own students but also by the presenters.

For the sophomore American Literature curriculum, the activity offered students at that time in the year an opportunity to examine authentically the concept of the I/We Paradox, prior to heading into a unit on the American Dream, so the connections would help to deepen classroom investigations. My whole career as an English teacher had been based in a confidence in inquiry. To break down the walls of the classroom and connect one's self to the world, both inside and outside of our classrooms, is to make one's learning more meaningful and dance like a wave of the sea. It means to be moved by one's education. It stays with you.

Well, yes, you were still elementary-aged students in 2008 during this Bead Activity. At that time, many students kept the beads visible, some on their backpacks, others on their wrists, for some time to come, serving as a reminder of a commitment to social justice in their communities and their ability to affect positive change. Because they did not simply sit back in a classroom only filling in worksheets or only writing essays that only a teacher would read, they were deeply learning in connection to their community—to their friends and classmates. They engaged a powerful passion for inquiry.

Because they did not simply sit back in a classroom just filling in worksheets or only writing essays that only a teacher would read, they were deeply engaged in their own learning that was connected to their community—to their friends and classmates. They engaged a powerful passion for inquiry.

The pendulum, of course, then swung back, as it tends to do in life. An especially vibrant and skilled colleague had begun a Gay-Straight Alliance. Now seemingly back in a more public acknowledgement of inclusion, I remember faculty members had emerged from their chrysalis as allies. Rainbow stickers alighted on classroom doors and over whiteboards, and other visible spaces so students clearly knew where they could comfortably be themselves. Mine stood proudly on the window of our classroom door for many years while I taught English at South Winsor High School. I was thrilled to support all students in the classroom to read, write, talk, question, and ultimately enter the conversation of the world of ideas that inspire people to adopt life-long learning practices. We know, then, that conditions for a confidence in inquiry exist.

You might have heard about a time at South Windsor High School when several students wore T-shirts to school that read, "Adam and Eve, not Adam and Steve." I starkly remember when students wore those t-shirts to the high school. Whether or not a direct response to the establishment of the school's Gay-Straight Alliance, tensions became acutely public. The principal at the time called on the HRC to participate in a larger school-wide conversation that would be videotaped and made available to the public.

The then-Superintendent and the administration facilitated a school-wide discussion. That conversation broadened the issue to one of free speech, so that students from multiple perspectives and diverse backgrounds could take place. Racial tensions had also elevated the anxiety level of students at South Windsor High School, so those frustrations were also given voice. I remember my students serving on a panel, as a lawyer offered his interpretation of student rights as left "at the school house door" in public schools. They discussed, shared points of view, and otherwise engaged in the free discourse of ideas in response to legal interpretations and personal experiences. I remember, then, the school's tension level decreased given the conversation. No resolutions emerged, of course, as the homophobia that prompted the need for the conversation would explode later without discussion in my case. However, a very public and controversial topic was addressed by a community of learners, and the learning experience resonated above all else for most students and faculty. That passion for learning, in a world that is not painted black and white in opposites but rather is covered in swirling color, can sometimes confuse and even scare people. But, this event demonstrated that those fears can be reasonably and democratically addressed. I love the idea of learning as an attitude of openness—as a confidence in inquiry — with the persistence to examine those ideas, especially when they allow us a chance to discover that which had been hidden.

My own teaching of thirty years was a move toward a live lesson in developing and forwarding understanding of others as worthy of acknowledging and addressing injustice—together, to be learners in a pluralistic democracy. Without the conversation on this page, you likely would never have known some of these experiences and extraordinary work that went on during your time at South Windsor High School on your behalf. Without the act of putting words to this page—to you—I would not have had the chance to share the stakes of a skill set of inquiry and engagement with the world. I'm warmed by this life work. My fingers are shaking as I type the words to you, "We can say that we included in our teaching the stuff of feeling human—of being honest and open, and inviting multiple ways of thinking." These are the waves of the sea, rolling on, forward into a future of learning for all.

Bus Language Spills into the Café

Well, it's 7:25 am one morning at the high school 1997. The final bell for first period has rung. I'm overseeing study hall in the cafeteria during Period 1 that semester. And, after the couple who are holding hands as they enter find their seats in the cafeteria, the doors will close, and everyone will have settled into Period 1 study. I'm sitting and working with a young teaching colleague on a reflection activity I had written earlier that morning at 5:30 a.m. at home. We open up the document, each on our own devices, to discuss the reflection. We had agreed to talk about creating learning reflections for our student readers, writers, and learners during this study period. However, a bit of a commotion would pop up at the door by the corner of the cafeteria, near the vending machine filled with apple, cranberry, and orange juice. Voices barked out; the door slammed; so, I headed over to check it out: several students were arguing.

I remember three students with our Hartford Choice program were upset. I remember the voices growling loudly. Two guys weren't hitting each other, but they were kind of bouncing off each other. There was physical contact, and a young lady between them stated pretty clearly that she'd had it, already.

As a Connecticut suburban school, South Windsor High School is obligated to educate all students and legislation was originally passed in 1997 to diminish an ugly racial and socioeconomic gap that has grown like a disease and persists in Connecticut schools. I strongly encourage you to look up the Sheff v. O'Neill case that sought to address this on-going problem. The black students who had applied and been accepted into the state-wide program – and were enrolled and attending South Windsor High School – get up earlier than most; travel farther than most; and, are individually unique. More, they are part of educational experience that brings them from one cultural milieu to another, from Hartford, CT to South Windsor, CT.

It was too early in the morning for this, I thought.
"'Morning," I interrupted. "Okay for us to sit?"
"Yessr. Sure."
I remember their visible frustration. One young man

tossed his backpack into the booth. They all sat. I slid up a chair and sat, getting ready to listen.

They grumbled. Something about the bus. Something about the front office.

The students sat slouched in frustration, stuffed into the small booth. Two students faced one another and the other faced me, all with their heads down and hoodies up. One of the students gazed out. Our eyes met. His frustration level beamed, as I recalled thinking about the recent response to the change in administration.

They told me the "N" word had been thrown about on the bus on the way to school, but it only exploded when it echoed off the walls in the foyer as the students dismounted the bus. The word was reported by another student already in school, and an administrator intervened in the foyer—the students on the bud from Hartford were taken into the office for interrogation. The boys claimed, to me, unfair treatment. They fussed that they had used the word in solidarity. In bonding. In playful and forceful banter. The young man contended, "No one in this school gets me!"

The others in the booth responded to the call, "Damn Straight."

Because, two of the three students I faced sitting at the end of the booth were seniors, and had been on the HRC, I asked if there were anything from the class that might help them think about this morning's situation. Did they see any connections? What seemed to be at work?

Silent fuming. Eyes pinned down. Heads heavy with the weight of alienation.

I pushed. "What about socialization? Who in your encounter this morning has been socialized to hold assumptions about the 'n' word?"

Still silent, fuming. Eyes still pinned down. Heads still heavy with the weight of alienation. I pushed again.

"What about socialization? Who in your encounter this morning has been socialized into prejudice?"

Silence. Tension.

Then, the young lady tilted her chin up. Raised her eyes. Spoke. "Well, I hear friends use that word. Some black people use it. So, I aks you, why can't that AP understand that? Why is he all up and down our backs?"

"The assistant principal must not understand that the school setting loads that word," I replied.

The other young man injected, "Well, in Hartford, we've been raised around it. But here. People have been taught it's…. it's, well, taboo. I'm sure the AP thinks that."

"Yeah, but who said his socializ' owns ours?" She countered.

One nodded. "It sucks. Language drags us down, but actually it's ours. It seems to shut us out sometimes. It draws lines."

"'Nuff to bust your crayons."

We sat in silence as that question lingered, and then we started laughing.

"Bust your crayons!!? Ah, Girl!"

Tension cracked! Tamara's creative language shook us all free as we sat in the booth. Fingers released themselves from fists and heads elevated a bit. We would not resolve this issue over the shifting values between one's initial socialization at home within our families, extended families, and in our neighborhoods, the ownership of words, or the power of language at this moment, but students seemed to agree think more about it.

As I think back on that five-minute exchange, I am

still worried by the challenges other students face in navigating the social and academic landscapes they occupy, especially when they are different, or their immediate cultural backgrounds are different from the majority of a community. And, as communities continue to diversify, even in new ways the term "diversity" has yet to acknowledge, more instances of contact happen. Students increasingly need to learn to listen to one another on a human level and adults need to model that attitude and skill set. However, adults who are stuck in a past set of their own socializations and refuse to acknowledge the silencing of difference, instead holding on to strict expectations of behavior, frustrate me because they reduce and debilitate students' sense of self-worth instead of bolstering and celebrating it. A needed sense of agency. For teachers, these are complicated human interactions that require supportive approaches. Credentialed teachers tend to live under deep-sea pressure to keep problems quiet, instead of negotiating cultural conflict in honest conversation and problem-solving, to prepare students as democratic citizens, respecting those in the public square. Too often, such as our situation back in February of 2015, administrators prefer avoidance of issues if not maintenance of the status quo. I always loved identifying and making visible room for discussion about difference. Dance, dance, dance!

After talking with the students, I got up and returned to work with my young colleague. We called up the document on my light blue clam shell MacBook.

"Don't hold me to it," I joked. "I wrote it at 5 am this morning."

As we finished, she asked about the tiff in the corner. I told her about the students' struggles as African Americans in a predominately white school with administrators who seemed to have treated them as a block when been brought into the office as a group. I told her, too, that I couldn't help but think of the work we were doing with the Culture and Diversity Fairs were as important as ever.

Culture Fairs

At this time in 1997, a transformation was happening with our student-empowered HRC, in large part, because of a student of Pakistani descent argued during a meeting after school that the committee should sponsor a multicultural fair. Embossed in my mind, her firm but gentle demeanor, which always drew the room's attention, beckoned the other students to consider the possibilities. As you all know, even as I write in this letter to you, South Windsor's population had changed and is still changing today. She said our community needed to invite the diverse students and their families from the Middle East, Asia, Caribbean, and South America into the conversation. In fact, the majority of the students meeting after school had last names of Shah, Chaudhary, and Randhawa, mixed with the African American names of Thomas, Johnson, and Stevenson. South Windsor was changing ethnically. This newly emerging student leader had visited several culture fairs within her own family network and found them exciting and educational. Her ideas lit a new flame in the hearts of our members, and the South Windsor Diversity Fair was born. Most all of you likely had attended this fair during your time at the high school—or at least had heard of it. Now you know it's beginning—and it's purpose.

I remember our first fair hosted student group presentations about six countries and their cultures: India, Pakistan, Jamaica, Sweden, Ghana, and Poland. What many people do not know is the enormous amount of time students devote to interests connected to the classroom, and the equally large chunk of personal time teachers offer to support their students in their interests. For as many teachers, there are generally twenty times the interests of students, who need to apply their own creative minds. For the next almost fifteen years, once a week after school, my colleague and I voluntarily served as advisors. This included time to plan and prepare for after-school sessions and to facilitate students' own learning about and spreading of their cultural curiosity within the school.

Students came to school early on the day of the first fair, with presentation boards tucked under their arms, cultural clothing draped over their shoulders, and parents in tow, helping with bags of cultural artifacts. They transformed the foyer of our school building into an enticing display of cultural values, beliefs and habits. Indian elephants and racks of bracelets adorned table tops, with Ukrainian nesting dolls next to a table filled with Hans Christian Andersen books. The area was colorful. It was noisy. It was a buzz of excitement. It was awesome.

After the first classes of students poured into the fair, I remember a Pakistani girl, with her face turned up, casually smiling to me, as I walked by: she was hand painting henna on another student's hand. She was dressed in a colorful sari, wrapped around her like a hug; her brown feet poked out from beneath her sari's base and her toes were painted colorfully; her black hair was pulled back tightly into a bun; and a pungent aroma floated about her. Those brown, art-colored hands appeared later throughout the school. The henna lasted for days as did the lingering excitement and respect for students who, for the first time at South Windsor

High School, took the risk to bring their own passion for learning and cultural knowledge to a predominantly white student body. The joy! The courage! We celebrated the differences of students—and students reveled in it.

That spring, the fair became a staple and was held by many as a premier event at the high school for the next almost fifteen years. A colleague joked once with his serious wit, "David, did the administration come to you again this year for the fair's attendance numbers to submit as the high school's entire diversity efforts to the state?" His wry humor aside, the students' work, which annually engaged over 1,000 students and forty faculty members became well-known both in the district and in town. Anticipation increased each year, as students' pictures painted the local paper with in the spring, with students mingling, dancing, and celebrating in color photos.

Over the years, my colleague and I sought to support the kids' energy, as the desire both to present a culture or attend the fair grew. Students' familial pride shined over those years. At its height, students presented over twenty-two countries, which dotted the inside of a 60' x 80' three-pole tent outside. Over one hundred students a year took part in planning, presenting, and cleaning up after a cultural celebration.

In fact, we even developed a relationship with Wapping Elementary School, situated next to the high school, through a third-grade teacher.

I remember the first time I met him through a Wapping Elementary colleague who had served as the Connecticut Education Association president. She had introduced us after I had gone to her with the students' ideas to connect with elementary school students, to share their

43

learning and love for diverse cultural experience. As student leaders in solving conflict, they planned to scale their work and offer an invitation to elementary students to attend. We had coffee one summer morning, and we shared our passion for opening space for all students to be themselves as they explored the world as learners. Black framed glasses sat snuggly over his neatly trimmed eyebrows. His eyes sparkled with enthusiasm. He spoke movingly about the challenges children faced when growing toward healthy adults, especially given continuing cultural intolerant attitude toward difference.

We agreed to a partnership. He helped gather elementary classes, while the high school presenters created cultural games and presentations for these young students to experience. For example, the high school students invented a project where the elementary students "travelled the world" with their passport made by the presenters. Elementary students gathered stickers after visiting each cultural booth and presentation. The idea to engage young students with difference at a young age resonated with everyone involved.

At a young age, elementary students are learning the habit of mind, upon which the confidence of inquiry may be built. This habit of mind is, of course, developmental, both cognitively and socially. It asks us to enter into the world as an individual and begin to see ourselves as a larger streak of light in the visual mosaic that is our world. As students develop as learners, it is essential that these perspectives be spoken. And, be heard. For us to inquire into the world, we must understand affectively that other points of view exist and are valid and varied. Those ideas of difference compelled not only the elementary students but also the high school students. While difference interests people, connections to one another in the sharing of knowledge draw people together: we see our similarities as human beings, and in that process we become more human. More understanding. More empathetic. More knowledgeable.

During the last fair in the spring of 2014, one student from Haiti, who had been adopted along with his two sisters by a South Windsor angel-teacher, especially touched many of those over 600 students and their teachers who voluntarily came to the fair. He had prepared a booth on the Haitian culture, from its history that included an eclectic mix of African and European elements. He beamed as he spoke in a mix of English and Creole about Henri Christophe, who was a leader in the revolt against France as Haiti won its independence in 1806. His timid posture gave way to his smiles and strong shoulders as he played the national anthem on his synthesizer recently given to him by his adopting mother. He had been rescued from an orphanage after his parents could not care for him amidst extreme of poverty. He survived the earthquake of 2010, and was he now presenting in America a vastly unique perspective.

These fairs invigorated the South Windsor community. What do you remember about them? A lot of students loved those moments. Not just because they got to get out of a class for an hour, which they did, but because they got a chance to see their classmates in a new light: rays of new light glinting off the gems that were their fellow students celebrating pieces of their own identities. Sharing them with the world. I hope you remember the celebration of multiple cultures and felt the sense of belonging, too, that helps create a climate for learning excellence!

The Diversity Fair offers us a longstanding example of the confidence in asking real question. Where are you from? What's your family history? What familial and cultural values do you hold? How does your family celebrate your cultural identities? How are we similar? How are we different? How can we value those similarities and differences as a community of learners? I draw upon the words I need to assemble this letter to you that illustrate an exploration into the cultural richness that thousands of students had been engaged—engaged into a world of ideas and conversation. I hope these words spotlight a democratic experience in your former high school. People's varied experiences are in front of us. We just need ask, and keep asking.

I know you are all keenly aware that high school can be very difficult, if not downright tortuous, for a range of reasons. High school's tough. A lot of changes in teenagers' lives. One particular sophomore student struggled mightily to fit into one of my American Literature courses. He appeared in my classroom in 2000 in physical presence only, really. The idea of inquiry in school seemed the farthest thing from his mind. He really struggled. Not only was he striving to communicate with others but just to find the words as a learner. Writing just disappointed him. And, frankly, I can relate. I found him a very bright young man who wrestled with social interaction AND with his pen, itself. His handwriting was legible only with a headlamp. His sharp, neurodivergent mind ran faster than he could lay ink or lead to the paper. He even winced with pain in class when writing. Speaking and writing were not working for him.

I remember a paper he had written on Rebels in America, which he attributed to a fascination with the concept of the American hero. He brilliantly had made the paradoxical connection between the two themes but of course was still wrestling with that writing tool, the pencil. At that time, I had just purchased a new laptop: a muted light blue, clam-shaped

Apple iBook. Steve Jobs had unfurled this product, in part, with the education market in mind, so its intuitive operating system and artistically shaped shell certainly fit my needs at the time. I had been experimenting with technology to advance teaching and student learning since 1996 when I first arrived at South Windsor High School. Down the hall, we had had access to a single computer lab with Apple IIe computers, more designed for the Business Department, but several colleagues and I saw an opportunity to support emerging readers, writers, and thinkers. Can you believe it, the first computer lab at South Windsor High School! You likely also didn't know that my work as an educator with technology would lead me to travel to Washington, D.C. in 2004 to the International Society for Technology in Education conference with two colleagues to explore work with electronic portfolios. It was at that conference where I would attend a session on Diigo, a social bookmarking site, that has supported my own collaborative work with colleagues. I dig the interconnectivity and possibilities for writers as collaborators! But students needed access!

After purchasing the laptop, I offered it to him for use, while the class drafted by hand. The eager young man took to the keyboard like a Labrador to water. I remember him raising his eyebrows and tilting his head in incredulous response to writing that appeared on the screen on the blue gem. His fingers pecked, one at a time, across the keyboard, and he took to a new writing environment. And it changed him. It changed his attitude, and it empowered his ability to write for various audiences, in all his classes. A stout young wrestler pinned into his student desk, he nevertheless engaged with the work of the class. His smiling face tilted up from time to time while tapping his fingers happily on the keyboard. He created drafts in class. Then, he began enjoying working in a group, sharing those drafts. He finished that year on the honor roll, and he went on to graduate and join the military. He and I would later talk after he graduated; he came back regularly to visit. We would chat about his wrestling, his interest in the military, and, of course, his own interest in technology. He excitedly chattered on about his experiences after high school. He had learned to chase his dreams.

I remember our school's principal calling me to his office at the beginning of the next year. I found my former students' parents next to the principal's desk. The father was standing, with his hands behind his back, and the mother was sitting with her hands folded in her lap. They both had serious looks on their faces. The father then burst into a smile, as did the mother, their faces beaming. The principal said, "David, these two have asked me to call you down here this morning to present a gift to you." The father held a very large book in his hand.

He opened the first of the 2,200 pages and read from the introduction: "I dedicate this book to David Olio who epitomizes everything good in an educator: professional, idealistic, and most importantly a fantastic teacher and mentor…the first to motivate my oldest son." Turns out, he wrote the first Microsoft Excel books. He had collaborated on and co-written *Access 2002 Bible,* the user manual for Microsoft's Access, a groundbreaking spreadsheet software at the time. He handed me a copy of a book, a framed picture of the cover that he signed, and a plaque, with the dedication written on it. I will always be grateful for the growth in my former student, not just engaging as an intelligent young man but also belonging in the class. Teaching means believing in all students and their abilities and figuring out the right support.

Students are capable. They are individuals. They deserve responsibility and trust to practice that responsibility.

Of course, the value of collaborative conversations is not new to any of you. You worked in groups in our classes for much of our seven months together. So, like a supporting section of paragraphs, I hope this section of my letter reveals the need for inquiry based in an integrity—an honest drive in the search.

. . .

So, this kid from Richmond is now in his 60th year of his own lifelong learning journey. I hope the letter speaks to you with words that fill in a bit of material not yet discussed. I feel as if I'm back in the woods again, if not for just a few moments, on this page. Assembling my own contribution to a conversation with you that should have been had ten years ago, in a way, breaks my heart. I just hadn't been able to speak to you.

So, yes. Let this letter and our public conversation sway like open meadows of brambles of blackberry and raspberry bushes that can feed a child for the day; more, let the classroom be a place of tree lined dense woods where are you enter the shade and cool air after being painted by the sun. Let the classroom be brooks of babbling water that zig and zag and carry leaves like little ships. Let our families be the woods to captivate and sustain our human souls and minds, and let the woods be an inviting community. Maybe these crafted metaphors help these words resonate. Let this letter open spaces for honesty, joy, and learning for you.

I said this assembly is crushing me, too. I have felt the inadequacy of my own writing. Hemmingway loved a short sentence that was true. And this is true, too: I did not take the ultimate risk when threatened with being fired over this poem. I settled with the district, ensuring my salary for a good deal later, to make sure we could pay for my son's last two years of college education. Those extra years of pay would enter me into a retirement pension. Although those turned out as important legal words for my family, they did not serve in the face of a then silenced public trial. It was a complicated and disturbing position the district put me in. I still don't know if I made the right decision. There's more to say about this. But I will say this: despite the sadness that this has taken me ten years to figure out how to write you, as much as it pains me that I could not figure this out earlier, I write and reinvigorate my own confidence in writing to animate the integrity of inquiry. I'm so glad to open and explore the world with you on this page.

I learned more about myself as a teacher while teaching and learned more about me and who I am in the world than I ever would have had I have not been an English teacher. I consider teaching a gift to this day. Thirty years of English teaching opened doors to ideas, histories, experiences, and feelings I never imagined, so this re-commitment to writing and learning grows for me again, despite the many challenges of the past and even those that face us all today. The word-honey feeds me, and life-long learning makes sweet sense. It requires much of us, so I we all need to lean into an honest inquiry. These words I offer you on this page inspired my practice—my professional approach. And, now, I offer you, again, words of devotion to learning.

4 THE INTEGRITY OF INQUIRY

You know, to talk with you in this letter, I feel full of gratitude. Writing empowers a full-throated and nuanced set of histories that inform a conversation, and I'm thankful to do that with you around my work. Teaching is not one of those jobs where you come home and toss aside your devotion until the next day. You inhabit experiences with students and colleagues, and they inhabit you. To engage a conversation about the robust context surrounding the Ginsberg reading in my AP/UConn ECE senior literature class—I seek to open the emotion As your learners together, let's open a window into my rock-solid belief in teachers and public education. Devoted English teachers don't simply read books because their curriculum says so but because as readers they are deeply aware texts are windows into a full range of human experience. They remind us of our humanity. But books don't simply sit on a shelf with some message in them we have to retrieve; educated readers bring themselves into a world of questions and connections. Authors have been read and reread for their artistic craft of sharing observations about the world. They empower us to push into the world, hold it up to the light, turn it like a gem to envision multiple points of views — and offer our own in return. I'm fortunate to have experienced thousands of perspectives in conversation among authors, their narrators, their characters, their critics, and other readers. Emily Dickinson calls books, "frigates":

There is no Frigate like a Book
To take us Lands away
Nor any Coursers like a Page
Of prancing Poetry –
This Traverse may the poorest take
Without oppress of Toll –
How frugal is the Chariot
That bears the Human Soul –

And upon these seas I have sailed. I'd like to take you to 1996, when I was first hired. My first South Windsor Public Schools Superintendent conducted a final interview with me for a position as an English teacher at South Windsor High School. I had been teaching for three years at another high school after finishing my student teaching at SWHS. As a result, I would be returning to the school where I had cut my teaching teeth, if I were hired. I remember sitting face-to-face with him at a small, circular desk in a generally well-kept office in the district's administrative building. We were talking about my recent teaching and books. I remember the conversation well — and it was indeed a conversation: we were sharing the books we had been reading at the time. With Boston accent coloring his words, he told me he had been reading Yeats, out of a healthy interest in the Irish and their literature. He stood up while asking if I had read the poet's work. He selected a hard copy from a row of books neatly waiting on his main desk and brought it back to our conversation. He asked me to choose a poem from *The Wind Among the Reeds* to discuss. I flipped through the pages and settled on the "Fiddler of Dooney." He asked me to read from that poem and talk with him about it. I remember our conversation about Yeats as a great Irish poet, about the role of poetry and art in our lives, and about the fiddler of Dooney, who, because of his craft as

an artist, inspired people "to dance like a wave of the sea." I
have always felt learning should be meaningful for individuals,
and I remember telling the Superintendent I hoped to inspire
my students to dance like waves on the sea.

He offered me the job, and I gladly took it; I was
excited to continue learning my craft; I was beyond excited to
engage learners; and I was intent on honestly exploring what it
meant to be human. In this way, I'd like to emphasize the
phrase, "integrity of inquiry." Beyond the sheer act of learning
as discovery, I believe teaching hinges on valuing inquiry as a
guidepost. Against the tides of the time that seem to accuse
teaching as some kind of political brainwashing or intent to
otherwise instill a social worldview, inquiry with integrity
disrupts unexamined assumptions and patterns of thinking.
Not for the sake of destruction, but to see new ways of
thinking. In this way, reading and writing are tools to think…
Indeed, as a newly hired English teacher, I was excited to
contribute to a profession whose purpose, I thought, included
inspiring students as learners, engaging students with language
to think, and preparing them to live thoughtful lives in our
pluralistic, democratic society. The world of ideas was open,
like a window open to a warm summer breeze. I looked
forward to examining ideas with you, my students. I can hear
a voice drifting and wafting over me from the "Fiddler of
Dooney." For when the artist plays his "fiddle in
Dooney/Folk dance like a wave of the sea;/For the good are
always the merry,/Save by an evil chance,/ And the merry
love the fiddle/And the merry love to dance."

Instead, after having taught for almost twenty years in
the English Department, a tempest in February 2015 blew
over the classroom with accusations that would eventually
burn the oxygen from the air. Ironic, isn't it, that I was first

hired by my first Superintendent for a cold, first reading of a poem, and then I was separated from my position and career as a secondary English teacher by the last superintendent I had for the very same act: discussing a poem after a cold reading.

To lean into that cruel irony and continue to give our conversation in this letter the oxygen we had been denied, I'd like to bring us back to 2010.

Silence is the tightly knitted fabric that can drown our human experience, so our lives have long been a fertile ground for writers who listen. Even English teachers, who have had access to the pantheon of texts read by millions over time are subject to the quieting narratives of their time. I feel as if our time in 2014 to 2015 signaled an especially dangerous era, where push back against the growing acceptance of traditionally marginalized groups burst into flames. I believe justice threatens those more favored in comfortable positions of social and institutional power. Despite this pushback, my own life reflects an American sense of optimism amidst the degradation of our human selves. It may sound saccharine, but I believe in joy and optimism. They never really leave me.

My joy in the world met a new craft as I joined the South Windsor High School English Department. I remember choosing the district in which I would student teach earlier in 1992. I was finishing my certification program after I had first decided to become an English teacher in 1989, leaving a sales and marketing job with a company in Massachusetts: I had selected to live in central New England after college, as a result. I moved to Middletown, CT, after attending Saint Michael's College and took a job. While living working on my own for the first time, I had taken a course at Southern Connecticut State University that changed my life. I know, who takes a Medieval Lit course for fun?

The Medieval English course hadn't just presented chronological lists of ballads, lais, fables and lyric poetry, but it unpacked chivalric romance in terms of authority, among many other themes and forms of the era. I remember the course raising questions like, who even gets to be a hero? What expectations do the people who deem others as heroes have? In what ways does the heroic fulfill our expectations for people's roles in our society? The discussions were amazing. They reignited a joy of learning in me that I frankly had missed out with during my first degree in Business Administration. As I write to you about this seminal course that triggered a change in career—from sales and marketing to education—I'm aware of the ways audience and language has shaped me. Writing to you now reminds me of the tensions between the vernacular, or common every-day-letter-writing language and the formulaic and poetic forms of Medieval Chivalry. Some strict religious codes were carried by that language way back when, and now the more informal tone of a letter (like to you) has the chance of freeing my story to emphasize an integrity of inquiry and honesty about our learning. I hope to harness this letter writing form. A voice has already emerged in this letter, I hope! It took me years to find and choose this form to finally carry my words to you.

Well, once I returned to school at Central Connecticut State University for a degree in teaching Secondary English, I had had a choice where my student teaching would occur toward the end of my program. Don Gallo, my amazing university supervisor, nationally known for introducing English departments across the country to Young Adult Literature (YAL), offered me a choice: a more traditional English department in a larger district or an

English department on the cutting edge.

Wait a minute. Even those words "Young Adult Literature" I discovered carry a history of good trouble and deserve at least a few words here. You might not know, but the vast majority of short stories taught in high schools prior to 1986 were not written in younger voices about subjects immediately important to young adults. Everyone in high school used to primarily read about adults—or, at least adults talking about the world. Older people. It wasn't until this golden era when Don published the first book of short stories *about* and *for* young adult readers. Sure, there had been children's books, *Adventures of Huckleberry Finn*, and some stories by Ronald Dahl and Edward Stratemeyer, but most of those—except, of course *Huck Finn*—were not considered serious enough for reading and learning in high school English Departments. As a student here at the high school, however, you would have been exposed at least to *Huck Finn* if not other YAL books. I'm appalled as I think back on the growth of this literature that the last ten years has seen a skyrocketing of attempts to ban books in this genre. We'll get to this a bit later.

Well, Don told me I would learn a lot through either choice as he explained the two different programs. The first option would teach me classroom management especially, but the latter might spring into something special—a revision of curriculum based not simply on chronological survey of genres but on students as learners, using reading and writing as tools for thinking was underway; so, I needed to decide who I was going to be as a teacher based on who I was as a learner. In the traditional setting, I would likely continue with traditional curricula centered on classic books, but the other I might be able to introduce the English department to new voices such as those in Don's book and be part of creating learner-centered curriculum. I chose a gorgeously fateful path.

Of course, the joy I had felt of learning something new of challenging the world was now fiercely growing in me, so I chose the South Windsor High School English department. The department had embarked in the mid to late 1980s on a revisioning of learners. Instead of seeing kids and chairs and desks as recipients of information they were exploring this democratic idea of individuals within communities shaping their own meaning in the world.

The experience blew my mind. It excited me. I felt alive in joining this department of teachers who were researching, writing, and redesigning learning environments, a lot on their own time. Student-centered learning blossomed in many classrooms. You may not know this, but the South Windsor High School English department was recognized in 1986 by the National Council of Teachers of English as an award-winning department focused on redesigning curricula with reading and writing as tools for thinking and learning. These teachers geeked out over the idea that students were centered in the process of learning. They had a voice in the work of the classroom, rather than only being told what's important to give back on a test. It's a tenet of twenty-first century habits of mind, as economic, social, and democratic citizens.

I remember telling our student-teaching group who met at Don Gallo's house about the revision of sophomore American Literature, shifting from teachers summarizing stories, poems, and novels in chronological order to the presentation of texts as places of inquiry into American ideas and habits ideas. What does it mean to be American? What does it mean to be an individual? What does it mean to be an individual within a community? What does the American Dream mean? What does the American Dream mean to those who have not had access? My fellow student teachers were blown away by these questions as organizing ideas. Imagine the change from being told what an Emily Dickinson poem supposedly meant to asking the question what does the narrator tell me about the idea of longing in an American community?

> Much Madness is divinest Sense -
> To a discerning Eye -
> Much Sense - the starkest Madness -
> 'Tis the Majority
> In this, as all, prevail -
> Assent - and you are sane -
> Demur - you're straightway dangerous -
> And handled with a Chain —
>
> Emily Dickinson

The narrator's ironic phrase, "Much Madness is divinest Sense" opens the door to myriad ways of thinking about writing, about communities, about individual longing for freedom of thought. In this way, I hope you see in this letter an educational design for you and other students over the years to truly engage in authentic, inquiry that moves us from one understanding to another. It's not surprising that still so many people believe that teachers are trying to somehow brainwash students into thinking one way or another, if they see learning as simply a delivery system for an institution. The very idea of thinking about the world and ourselves as an ongoing process counters a way of thinking that information is simply delivered from teacher to student.

Many still view schools as a way of delivering

information, including static cultural information, but I've never held that view as an educator. I aimed to help students explore new ways of thinking through multiple points of view about the world. Students get to make their own choices— and, as an intellectual move, choosing includes evaluation, synthesis and creation, higher orders of thinking. I always wanted to know what students thought about others' perspectives—and thus their way of approaching an idea.

But, the South Windsor English Department I would join had been envisioning and launching a cutting-edge and inclusive approach to learning already. It's tough to write these last sentences because they sit on the verge of disciplinary jargon, so I'll craft the words more directly here: the act of learning is for students to own, and the department had decided to honor this most fundamental principle. Think about it: in classes where students sit in rows, as they did under traditional approaches, students have been considered vessels to fill with utilitarian facts and cultural knowledge. My own experience in school fell under this approach. Remember that little boy earlier in my letter, with his lil' hands waving in the air, waiting to give back the answer? That was a student of the distant past in training for the distant past. Sit. Get. Wait. Give back. Repeat. So, given my own experiences in school, the idea of engaged learning I felt happened while I was in the woods, discovery rushing through my veins. The South Windsor English Department did not fail to deliver. Blew me away.

So, our classes were not about assenting but demurring. This was exciting revision that had been happening in the South Windsor English Department prior to me joining and after. Students were sitting in circles, so they could talk to each other. So they could listen to other points of view different from their own. So they could have a wide variety of perspectives that represent the fabric of the American democratic quilt. So they could then stitch their own thinking into an ongoing conversation. That feeling I told you about earlier when I was out in the woods in Sherborn, Massachusetts—and keep reminding you about— well, this is the joy that I felt entering this English Department. The excitement!

However, I believe Dickinson's narrator says out loud what's close to my chest: truth and much madness is divine sense, and that concept helps add more context to my struggle to write you over the past ten years. At the time of our class I had demurred to the prevailing notions about sexuality. We had put our eyes and ears on some electrified poem, held impermissible by the "majority." And, as the narrator warns, they handled me with a chain. I hope we can discuss these words. I guess I should not have been surprised, but I was committed to the integrity of inquiry into books, poems, and stories expressing nuanced, complex, and challenging ideas about our lives. So much faith. The rejection was heartbreaking.

But those almost twenty years spent with my colleagues, with students, and with families are primary, over the secondary experience of the chain and the pain it inflicted. I remember a photograph I had taken of our classroom. Four of you face each other in a small group in one of my sophomore American Literature classes. Student artwork from presentations and projects, posters of characters from novels like *Adventures of Huckleberry Finn*, and stickers of quotes from authors like George Orwell, one reading "In a time of deceit, telling the truth is a revolutionary act," cover the wall behind you. Just in front of the colorful wall stand our writing table, on which milk crates containing student folders sit ready to empty out printed student writing for exchange during the writing process. You are sharing ideas. Talking about and exploring the world. The four desks turn each of you to face another. One of you have your hands stretched into the air; another sprawls their leg out to the side. It's a picture of four of you reveling in your learning.

One's mother had worked in the main administrations office. She had told me that you really loved this English class, even though you weren't really "a reader." You weren't one of those students who had grown up with a book in your hand but rather a lacrosse stick. You're a great kid who enjoyed learning, though. I had chatted with your mother on one of the many days I had been in the administrative office, whether helping to plan professional development for the high school, middle school, or one of the five elementary schools. I served as a member of multiple committees for the district, even co-chairing the district's Teacher Evaluation and Professional Development Committee at one point. Your mom told me about conversations at home you had about the books we had been reading and discussing and writing about.

The English department more than imagined those families whose students struggled to fit in. We worked with them. We wrote curriculum that explored, for example, The I/We Paradox. Struggling to be one's own individual person, we are inherently tied to our communities. We're not solely independent. We wrote to explore important themes of becoming life-long thinkers and learners and to prepare students to know they individually matter and know they are an important part of this process in the school. I know I don't have to tell you about the difficulties in high school. So many students struggle with mental health, especially wondering if they belong or how they belong or don't belong. I'm sure most of you know about the isolation. The English Department's curricula invited students to take part in conversations. We designed work wherein people could be themselves and drive the work of the classroom.

In this way, challenges always emerge when you're engaged in honest, full-throated conversation, and this is important if we are to nurture and sustain those conversations. They make some people uncomfortable. And, the English Department experienced this as a group in the early 2000's when an African American family in South Windsor challenged the inclusion of Adventures of Huckleberry Finn in our sophomore curriculum, which had been selected to serve as an important text in the conversation in a unit of study titled: "The I/We Paradox" in sophomore American Literature.

I'd like to focus frame this with you, in my letter, as an important learning moment for teachers. We discussed, at least, the importance of helping students with the cultural and historical context of the language—and the stories it tells.

After much discussion, our department chair arranged for a conversation to teach with the novel more supportively, especially after the banning that had occurred in New Haven, CT just a few years earlier in the mid-1990's. As reported in the New York Times article, "Learning to Teach the Book," some parents and their high school-aged students have had more than just negative reactions to the "N" word. Some find it downright irresponsible, to subject students of color to the language that has been part of so much injustice in the past and present. The former English teacher and Harvard English professor leading the workshop at the Mark

Twin House in February of 2000 offered strategies that cited the need to support students' development of their own thinking and feeling. Michelle Murphy, who writes *The New York Times* article, quotes Professor Jocelyn Chadwick saying,

"'You have to gird up your loins, walk into class, pick out the strategic chapters, the controversial passages, and read them aloud. Take them through a deep read. Help them peel back the layers. Make them understand that the word 'nigger' is troublesome because of the meaning it has today. At the time Twain wrote this, that was the operative term for slave, in the south. And Twain is striving for realism in this book."

I especially like Chadwick's approach to "peel back the layers," as I'm trying to do here with you, in this letter. Yes, it does seem to be my memoir, and I think it is. Writing has a way of teaching us as we expose the many layers of disregarded, distorted, or obfuscated (sorry, another AP word!) meaning. We reassemble our words in relation to a reading or an idea and make new sense. Add a new idea. Create now. Just as I'm doing in this letter to you. Writing is not simply an exercise in taking something out of your head and communicating it on the page; instead, we learn when we write. We learn by finding those more precise words that speak back to us and even offer us new truths.

To understand the term "at that time" is to read critically; to recognize the existence of multiple perspectives that existed (and may even continue to exist) before the text, during the text, after the text. It's important to recognize, additionally, the many multi-layered perspectives that exist now. Just as this is true for each of you reading my letter. I certainly don't aim to persuade you about anything. I will note that open dialogue and honest inquiry can lead to difficult and challenging conversations, including those about oppressive histories and denigrating habits of our present. I firmly believe a shared sense of purpose in the integrity of inquiry and honesty of learning may counter the attempts of silence when it comes to books in the public square. We must avoid urges to censor language or books.

5 ALTERNATE VOICES

I remember in 2011 walking through my old classroom doorway as the bell rang to begin 6th Period, my Alternate Voices class. It was an unusually warm, late March day. So warm, that even the open windows on one side of the room had little cooling effect. The air was still. Humid. The blinds were drawn low enough only to leave enough space for some air to scratch its way over the sill and crawl into the room. The sun could be brutal through that wall of windows. The twenty or so students were dressed as if summer had not only been going for months but also had reached the dog days of August. Cut-off shorts, tank tops, flip flops, and pony tails dotted the desert landscape of the room. The lights were off. A fan whirred. The air still sat unmovable, like a shoulder against a closed door. It was very quiet.

We had been working on a unit of study in this senior elective class, which offered an inquiry into especially unique perspectives as readers, writers, and thinkers. Examining conscientious objectors, for example—a perspective rarely given breath in a country that has fought so many wars. Citizens who sacrifice their lives for democratic freedom deserve the respect and conversation about those wars in which they have fought and died. One young man sat erect, stiff-backed. Formal. Close-cropped hair cut. Neatly pressed t-shirt. Both of his hands stood in attention on the desk, one wrapped over the other, enclosing and guarding the other in a fisted shape.

Having taken a course with me for seven months in 2015, you may have heard me talk about of this upperclass course. You likely had knowledge of my work at South Windsor High School creating spaces for conversation from all perspectives. I mean, the Culture Fair had become an annual event that students loved—whether it was to get outside under the tent for an hour, as some of my teaching colleagues joked—or whether it was the excitement of the varied and unique expressions of cultural heritage and pride. And, we were designing courses such as Senior Honors that met students at the cross-roads of senior year and adulthood, pressing on more complex questions of readers' knowledge of their own sense of contributions to notions of Truth and the reading and writing process itself as theme of relationships. Course and activities were designed with students' engagement in mind. In other words, you likely were aware that an educational experience in room 147 was unique in some way—at least in a way that valued the energy of listening to new perspectives and the new horizons that emerge from the vibrant fabric that is each or us in the world.

You may have even had heard about the Alternate Voices class opened to juniors and seniors. It was an optional course offered by the English Department, along with other choices such as Drama, Rhetoric, Creative Writing, and Female-Male Perspectives. One might observe that the course Alternate Voices and Female-Male Perspectives are no longer available. Courses change.

In this course, though, in 2015, students read texts that featured common knowledge toward each issue. Students would identify and respond to those perspectives. Raise their own questions. Offer their own connections. Share their own evaluations. Then students read new perspectives not typically mainstreamed in the conversation. Authors provided unique perspectives, to which students offered their own thinking, as a result. They evaluated points of view, judged facts and conditions they deemed important, and then proposed and created projects to bring their own unique points of view to bear on the discussion.

The young man sitting next to the door clearly had a question that March day. As I walked past him on my way into the room, toward the middle of the circle structuring our work, he leaned toward the front of his desk. He leaned back. Then he leaned forward again and raised his chin. He had something on his mind.

And, before we even started, he broke the quiet, thick air, and asked: "Olio, Can we get a guest speaker to come? I've been spending time at the Recruiter's Office. You know. There's respect in that office. Respect for our country. Respect. You know. Be all you can be. I've been thinking a lot about joining. We've been talking about conscience, and mine's been pumpin'." He looked down and then back up. "And, yeah, I really think you should hear from my recruiter. I mean, we talk all the time about alternate perspectives, but we haven't heard directly from the army. I think we should. Can we? The army's been an 'alternate voice.' We talk a lot about other perspectives, but I have to be honest, when it comes to war and conscientious objectors, that's all we read. World War II objectors. The people in the Japanese internment camps and the other objectors. We read about Korean War Objectors and Vietnam objectors." He went on to describe the recruiting office, the recruiter in uniform, the posters on the wall, and the pamphlets he'd been reading.

As he spoke, I stopped, and turned toward him, listening. I took a breath. Inside my head, I wondered if the reading strategy of recognizing and considering the "common knowledge" in a conversation made sense to him. For sure, there's a flowing river of a general narrative about the necessity of war as common knowledge—and its many tributaries—that feed a growing river of beliefs. People make dominant claims about values that underscore a long-standing knowledge of war as an "unfortunate" necessity. Since the Revolutionary War, the United States has been through over 100 military conflicts. Looking at those wars from own view, one might focus on the idea of a military action about every 2.6 years for the entirety of our country. From another perspective, another might focus in those 100 wars that over 1.5 million Americans have given their lives in battle. The tone of my inner voice continued. The United States has tens of thousands of War Memorials, with over 1,400 in Gettysburg alone. We've noted that sheer number of cemeteries and parades that honor those who have fought and who have given their lives. I appreciated his question because we value inquiry. And I wondered.

So, I continued to listen to him. Clearly, he valued conscience and service. He had told us earlier in the semester during discussions about each student's own values, beliefs, and experiences about service. About his sense of service. He had been a cub scout, moving into scouting, earning badges, and making friends. He talked about his sense of community and his sense of commitment to those around him. I remember to this day him talking about his Eagle Scout project, helping to maintain and extend the pathways that had been built a decade earlier in the Donnelley Preserve, just across Sullivan Avenue in the meadows near the high school.

"Well? What do you think?" he finished.

"Let me see…" I replied.

I hope you all felt while in your English class with me that your voice was and is important. That YOU are important. All that combines to make you IS important. Because you ARE. You matter. And because you matter; your education mattered to me. You deserved it. Not just as a student but as a human being. Your community deserves you—and all of you and your contributions that you potentially can make, whether it was in our classroom community or in your family, or in town. We all need to live our authentic selves. But we can't be if we can't speak honestly to each other. If a decision is made to silence conversation, where one's thinking is stifled, then you have been failed—and I have failed you as your teacher. I hope you never felt that I failed you in this regard. I certainly failed to defend my own self in a way that kept me from teaching at South Windsor High School. I failed in that it has taken me almost ten years to find a way to speak to you honestly about individuality, about community, about justice, and about education. But I hope this letter has mitigated some of that; has begun to reveal a more complete perspective about the ways cruelty works and the conditions under which it thrives.

Well, I took time to investigate the student's request. In this Alternate Voices course, designed to examine multiple perspectives of seemingly rooted ideas and practices, I took his idea and shared it with two other colleagues who each had a section of the course. I told them about the experience and the idea I had to honor the student's idea and request. First and foremost, I respect students as people; I believe in students' rights, and I value them as their own person. I decided I would honor this request and pursue an in-person conversation with his military recruiter. In my mind, too, the experience could help sharpen and deepen the class's learning path of "common knowledge."

My colleagues were dubious but interested. Why not pursue a conversation? As we collaborated about the ways to go about a classroom conversation, it became clear to us that we need to construct the event *for a conversation.* One colleague knew of a speaker who had been visiting schools to talk about conscientious objection in legal, moral, historical, and personal levels. They would make contact to inquire about a visit and an engagement with the military recruiter. I would contact the local recruiter and inquire about a visit and an engagement in conversation with the peace advocate. Of course, I needed to discuss this with the principal to determine feasibility. I spoke with my department chair to organize materials and resources for the visit. As inquiry and collaboration developed—and excitement grew—over this class experience, it became clear this could be—and should be—a larger conversation hosted by the Alternate Voices classes. My student would help emcee.

Of course, the Gulf War had ended—do you remember the Gulf War?—but, the Afghanistan and Iraqi military conflicts were in full swing. The US committed people to battle and resources to support them. The country would end up spending over 2.3 trillion dollars, according to the Watson Institute. The conversation about war was also in full-swing. The US Congress passed a Memorandum of War unanimously, drawing upon common knowledge of using violence to solve our post-9/11 issues. This was an important conversation for my student. It was an important conversation for the seniors about to graduate and who were thinking of joining the armed forces and who must sign up with the Selective Service. It was an important conversation for our community. After all, our school helped to distribute

Selective Service registration cards, as all high school guidance departments do in the US for students turning eighteen.

So, I contacted the recruiter. We had already secured the other speaker. The initial conversation was formal and kind. I heard the recruiter speak of my student's visits, and he described him as a "good American." Then, he put me in touch with a colonel, who agreed to come himself to speak on behalf of the United States Military Recruiting office. I began making the arrangements to schedule the auditorium, including securing students from the Drama department to handle lighting and sound. I wrote the announcement to my colleagues, inviting them to bring students to the program that emerged from an Alternate Voices student—emerged organically out of the student's connection to his world and that of his classmates. Constructing these interconnected learning experiences for my students motivated me during my teaching career. I loved supporting students to extend and to deep their learning by applying to the many communities to which they belong. There's little more satisfying than facilitating meaningful learning experiences for students. In fact, I hope this letter inspires you to continue to extend your own personal and professional learning into new avenues. Making connections, applying your curiosity, and driving new thinking is the stuff of life-changing learning.

The morning of the program arrived. All was prepared. The students had been fired up the prior class, finishing their work practicing their roles in the program, writing questions, and preparing the presentation slides that would guide the conversation. Everything was in place.

At 6:05 a.m. that morning, the phone rang at my house. When I picked up the receiver hanging from the wall. I answered. "Hello?"

"Hello," a sharp, stern voice replied. "May I speak to David Olio?"

"That's me."

The voice snapped back in a sharp, respectful military tone. "I'm calling to inform you the colonel will not attend the program at South Windsor High School today." The staccato voice continued. "The United States Army does not take part in civilian debate programs. It is required neither by law nor regulation to engage in discussion whereby it may have to justify its purpose."

Taken back, I was about to ask a question how to work this out in some way when the voice finished, saying, "Thank you for your contact with the United States Army Recruiting Office. Good bye." Click.

Dial-tone Silence.

6 FEBRUARY 25, 2015: 12 MINUTES
BEFORE CRUELTY

Down the English wing of South Windsor High School, room 147 sits midway. It was Period 2, February 25, 2015—the last day of student presentations in a unit of inquiry titled, Voices from the Wilderness. The unit sought to explore poets' use of language. On this day, in senior AP/ECE, we would end the last twelve minutes of class listening to Allen Ginsberg read a poem on YouTube. Unless you were in that classroom, you likely would have heard about the reading only through vague news reports or rumors. Maybe you talked with someone from the class. I don't know. So, let's return to that class. I'll take you through it, as I recall it.

If you were one of my students in sophomore American Literature, you would have been reading and writing about the American Dream later in the day. However, if you were in the AP/ECE Literature class, you would have crossed the threshold from the hallway into our room at 8:45 am or so to find your seat in your "home group." Your groups were structured based on the poet each of you had been studying. You might remember having gone to the Media Center as a whole class three weeks prior, to browse books of poetry the Media Specialist and I had pulled from the stacks. You all had about eighty poetry books to look through and choose from.

The poets ranged from Sylvia Plath to Robert Frost, from Rumi to Blake. The poets also included Walt Whitman,

Marge Piercy, Nikki Giovanni, Langston Hughes, Charles Bukowski, among others, and, of course, Allen Ginsberg.

I had paraded the books of poetry on large tables, inviting you all to read in the library for the period, to skim, to watch march by, and to otherwise explore poets who especially interested you. A book of poetry was waiting in hopes you might wrap your arms around it so that it could inspire you. After all, you'd be devoting your precious life, time, and energy to this work inside and outside of class. I designed the unit to introduce students to a breadth of poetic possibility and to capture and inspire the students' poetic imaginations, as you learned to understand how a poet's style helps develop the poet's ideas: to examine the two dancing in unison.

Once each student selected a poet who moved them, each student would then immerse themself into the poet's world, read the entire chapbook over the next two weeks, select three poems representative of the poet's style and themes, conduct research, and prepare an eight-twelve-minute presentation for a small group comprising four students. We would have three class periods of presentations, where students would not only present but also then listen to and engage with three other presentations in the small group. So, during a class of presentations, students held a total of nineteen poems up to the light and marveled at them. We closed each class with reflection, appreciation, and some final comments, or if time allowed, honored a student's suggestion of a poem for the class to listen to aloud.

During our first class of presentations, one student, Steven, had been part of another student's presentation, Archer's presentation of Allen Ginsberg, along with the poem "Howl." Steven and Archer often debated, cajoled, or

otherwise reveled in books they were reading. Given he had
been reading, researching, preparing, and presenting Charles
Bukowski, he found Archer's work on Ginsberg especially
relevant, moving, and informative. He had many questions
during that first presentation. In fact, he was so inspired by
the poem and their presentation that he would later bring in
from home Ginsberg's *The Fall of America: Poems of These States*
to our class. He had gone on to read that book, in addition to
having read his own for the class, in addition to reading his
books we had selected together for his thesis project that had
begun at the beginning of the second semester, in addition to
the books he was reading for fun on his own. In short, Steven
is a student every teacher adores: motivated by ideas,
independent in his quest for them, driven by the love of
inquiry. Curious.

As the second of the three presentations concluded
the week before, Steven had come to me with a question
about Herman Melville's *Moby Dick*, which I had
recommended to him for consideration for his thesis work. I
had told him that the novel was one of the greatest novels
ever written, in my opinion, and is one of my own favorite
books. More, though, it was a book of fertile ground for hi
inquiry. Later, I would learn that his mother was giddy that
Steven had really begun to read more "classic literature" as a
result of the class.

While reading, he had been confused by a reference
foreign to him; he wondered about the Lazarus allusion
Melville crafts, outside of the Spouter Inn, as Ishmael arrives.
He has just decided to go to sea.

He inquired, "Mr. Olio. What's going on in this
paragraph? I don't get it? Who's Lazarus and why does he
appear here? What does this mean?" "This is crazy!"

I asked for him to hand me the novel. I re-read the paragraph that I had read multiple times before, of Melville's famous novel.

"That's an allusion, Steven. It's an allusion to the biblical figure Lazarus."

"What's an allusion?

"Spelled with an 'A,' not an 'I,' an allusion is a reference to another body of work or historical moment. Allusions are not literal but instead evoke the ideas, assumptions, and expectations associated with the image."

"Oh. Cool."

"Here, Melville seems to have placed a figure who was an outcast and a beggar in front of the Spouter Inn as Ishmael approaches. Remember, although he describes the inn, Melville has given his first-person narrator the ability to make such observations for Melville's purposes. As you know, Lazarus is also the figure whom Christ resurrected--brought back to life." Steven tipped his chin downward, lost in thought. "You'll want to ask yourself, Steven, what does this allusion suggest for you? What developing ideas do you have that are deepened or modified or challenged by it?"

Steven titled his head up, still lost in thought. The bell rang. The class was over. "Thanks, Mr. Olio. That helps a lot. I didn't really know what an allusion was. Cool. See you tomorrow!" And Steven bounced out of the room with the other students in a flood to their next class. He would bring this same lively curiosity to our presentations and their discussions on this, our last day of the poetry unit.

On February 25, 2015—this last day of presentations, one student had selected and would present Mary Oliver. Another would lead discussion around William Blake, Yet another Percy Bysshe Shelly, and one, I think, Richard Wilbur.

You were engaged in a jigsaw activity.

After the clamor of settling in into the room at the beginning of a class, there was a special buzz. You had been talking together about poetry, and this was the last day of the presentations in the unit. As I look back on my notes I made the day after, I notice I had written, "There was a whizzing and whirling in the air." Yeah, we had started the class with our regular "Quick Chat" about the AP exam, practice thinking; but, more importantly, you were on the cusp of finishing a lengthy study of poetry.

Your notebooks plopped onto desk tops as you slid into your seats. Backpacks nestled aside your desks on the floor. The buzz emerged from your developing confidence with the language and very idea of poetry—or expression with language that barks or whispers or laughs at the human experience. But, we would be challenged in this class, in ways that none of us would imagine. We would find ourselves in a poem that pushed the very boundaries of poetry itself, and we would lose our center. We would succumb to its power.

So, the small groups became the world of each poet. In each group you would hear some background about the person examining the poet's role. You might have heard about the poet's birthplace or teen years. The presenter, of course, had prepared selected research as part of a larger story about the writer as a poet and language-builder. You likely would hear about the cultural conversation—or zeitgeist—of the era and maybe even some history. And as I write to you now, I remember the snap in the air our presenters brought for they had honed their work during this inquiry. You all had developed a bit of a feel for poetry. Questions were more targeted, research more tailored than simple summary, and your confidence had grown. More, there was also a certain excitement in conclusion: the unit was coming to an end that day. For those of you from my other classes, you may notice the cycle of the class. You folks had our classes rhythms down. As I reflect on your work, I'm grateful for these moments of collective work—striving together amidst the challenges of high school..

After the first round of presentations, the presenters would change, so the group would engage with the next poet. Each would bring their presentations to the next collaborative conversation with even more experience under their belts from the first presentation. This next group and a conversation, of course, addressed more than just the poet's background and their life; presenters analyzed, evaluated, judged, and connected to their work. The presenters would steer their audience to several seminal works that represented stylistic moves the presenter had determined were important — and then draw some conclusion about that writers ideas. We were looking for unique, fresh expression that brought the reader into an idea they hadn't heard before. Something that was stunning. Something kick ass.

Students in this small group heard about Mary Oliver's description of the human body as a spiritual connection. And then the next presenter would soar with William Blake's construction of Christian-based mythological worlds that dazzled the imagination of the human form. The two poets we're working with shared similar themes in such unique ways. So, the presenters were touching on this and other language, and the groups responded to the language and style with questions and connections to their own poets. I recall students presenting in moving language of their own — such newly constructed language! The presentations hummed.

When the 3rd and 4th rotations finished, a sense of

finality hung more noticeably in the air, and as I write to you about this work I'm teary eyed. To engage high school students in language that carries the complexity of human experience and to have watched your developing intellects wrestle with each poem moved and continues to move me. Whether you were a sophomore at the time reading this now in your mid 20's or whether you were a senior in one of my AP classes, our classroom was always a place for the breath of a voice speaking to the world. Emily Dickinson was right, I think, when she wrote, "How frugal is the frigate that carries the human soul." I'm really happy for your experience.

So, the presentations ended. High fives abounded. We had about fifteen minutes left in class for our reflective talking, thinking, and writing.

And as you sat in your groups, with the poetry of four poets on your breath, I looked up at the clock. I believe it was 10:48: 12 minutes before the end of Period 3.

I walked over to a particularly animated group of poet enthusiasts. Senior students in AP/ECE tend to hold deeply passionate feelings about the arts, whether it's drama, short story, poetry, pastiche essay (or better known as the collage essay). I approached a group of clear chatterboxes.

As I neared, one student popped up and said, "Mr. Olio! You can't believe what I found! I have this book of poetry by Allen Ginsberg and the language is crazy." Steven thrust the book toward me, and I don't remember very much detail about it, as I think back. I mean, usually I remember books' bindings, covers, images on the back matter. The feel of the page, the smell of the open text. The font. However, I certainly do remember my student's enthused interest.

I think it's important I restate in this letter to you, to add emphasis, that this student's interest had piqued during the Ginsberg presentation the week before. I have drafted this paragraph for us many times. In fact, I'm reminded that a first draft is a leap into the unknown, with waves of discovery in each revision. The revisions here, in this paragraph, led me to the initiating interest, where a mind first notices and pays attention. Mary Oliver writes that "attention is the first act of devotion." So, I repeat in revision: another classmate had included the poem "Howl" in their presentation and had wonderfully presented Ginsberg and his style with granular insight, placing Ginsberg in the conversation about the dehumanizing effects of American mainstream conformity. They also noted, as a result, the controversial nature of Ginsberg's oeuvre, and of "Howl" specifically. As an artist he challenged many American practices, including rigid gendered norms that undermined the individual and their contributions to community-making. His forms generally reflected his admiration for individual and local rather than traditional forms. These are my words describing Ginsberg's work. He worked with American poetic traditions, used by writers such as Walt Whitman and Herman Melville. His language was genuine, common, and unfiltered. Many critics characterize him as an acclaimed American poet and a leading figure in the Beat Generation. They noted his work is widely read and unpacks issues often ignored or even speciously generated by a "mechanized" American society.

His piqued interest in Ginsberg's work led him bring Allen Ginsberg's book *The Fall of America: Poems of These States* (1973), which had won the National Book Award, with him to class that day.

As I was walking to the chatterbox group, Steven raised the Ginsberg's *Fall of America*, went on to tell me he was amazed by the language, especially in one specific poem —

that it could be so "bad."

"Bad?" I asked. What do you mean by "bad?"

"You participated in a presentation on Ginsberg's work that covered a lot of his language that challenged the status quo, that sought to speak to America while working within traditions of poetic forms. His work was smack dab on the doorstep of the '60's, which challenged America's involvement in several wars, conformity of social beliefs about sanity, and our roles as Americans in our communities. You heard his poem "Howl" was the subject of the Supreme Court's ruling on obscenity. Remember?"

He returned. "I dunno. It's crazy." He waved the book of Ginsberg's poem around as he spoke.

I asked him, "Are saying the language is gratuitous? Without purpose?"

And we continued for a moment. He handed me the book. I flipped through to the poem in question, "Please Master." I gave it a cursory read. It was graphic. I saw language not commonly encountered in high school. However, Ginsberg is a major American poet, essential to the poetic and literary understanding of the late 1950's and 1960's.

I hadn't seen or read the poem before, but I did recognize a learning moment. And this was it. A class just finishing the story of poetry and language. Seniors in high school, about to graduate and go on to college.

I must admit to you now, as I look back on this moment, as I have hundreds of times, that I wasn't really thinking about justifying a reading of a poem aloud as a class. I wasn't really thinking about the school's policy that every student in a class would have to be over eighteen to listen to Ginsberg read his own poem on YouTube, as about half of the students or so who were still seventeen, on the verge of eighteen. I wasn't really thinking a broglio would unfold. I was thinking about this student's curiosity and his deep interest and questions about language. I was engaged in the joy of discovery that is learning that's integral to the classroom.

My student had been so passionate for and motivated by our class inquiry that he brought a book of poetry in from his home. Turns out his parents had previously brought Ginsberg's Fall of America back from a visit to Paris. The young man read pretty much everything in the house.

And he was animated by this poem. Of course we'd engage the integrity of inquiry!

So I looked him and said, "Let's hear the poem. We've got 12 minutes left in class. Can you look it up on my computer on the desk?" He did. And right quick. It came right up in the search. He would find the poem at poetry.com. While Steve was working at the teacher desk, I turned to move toward our classroom door to close it, saying that we needed to be respectful of others. And respectful of our public education. We did not want harsh language just floating our into the hallways. We didn't want this language just echoing down the halls.

As I turned toward the door, I focused the class' attention and sought to contextualize the poem we were about to hear—and to consider the question about gratuitous language. A cool inquiry for us all to finish this unit of study as students of literature and writing.

"I'm sure you all remember the strong presentation and discussion about Ginsberg's work last week. You remember the controversy around his poem "Howl." Well, we have another Ginsberg poem Steven has found at home." We had wrestled during the year with a wide range of language. Our study of the pastiche essay from, for example, included difficult language about the Holocaust as we worked our way through Susan Griffin's fifty-page pastiche essay, "Our Secret." Her work personally and creatively addresses issues of memory, war, history, Nazism, sexuality, homosexuality, familial betrayal, gender, healing, and art. The course design intentionally exposes students to complex ideas, with multiple strands, through literary forms that, too, operate with multiple genre strands. Griffin's essay, part her memoir—part image, part historical narrative, and part science report required the students to wrestle with the language and wrestle with the meaning. In that process, as readers, writers, and thinkers we had to contend with our own histories and our own images of identities. Griffin's unique style of the pastiche essay had opened us as a class to the silences that perpetuate injustice within families and communities and histories—an important beginning to the year in thinking about the role of writing for human beings.

Of course, there were other texts that opened difficult subjects, ranging from Sophocles' *Oedipus Rex*, where King Oedipus must confront his fated path to murder his father, marry his mother, have children with her, and then come to understand that in his ironic attempt to avoid the same prophesy that his life would end up following. We reveled as a class in each other, learning to close-read the language of fate, to examine dramatic irony, to marvel at the characterization in the undoing of a king and the birthing of a myth made famous by Sigmund Freud. We worked our way honestly through texts like *The Tragedy of King Lear*, wondering if deep pain is the most shared of human emotions--and the most necessary. I especially remember a discussion we had about the Elizabethan's Wheel of Fortune. We grew together as a class, learning to talk to one another with respect so students could challenge each.

I closed our classroom door. As I returned, I stood in between a planter on the window sill and back-of-the-room white board to listen to Ginsberg read the poem. I continued.

"Ya know, we don't want this to be 'a quote-un-quote AP incident.'" We want to consider Steven's question surrounding language. Does and/or how does the poet use the language purposefully—and to what poetic end?"

"Do you remember the conversations during Archer's presentation last week, that Ginsberg's work addressed an oppressive authority of American cultural habits and beliefs over Americans—and his work spoke about that oppression of authority? Ginsberg was passionate about belonging in communities and was adamant about giving voice to the barbaric yawp that Walt Whitman had screamed from the rooftops of the world in the 1850's?"

The Smartboard upon which we would watch Ginsberg was difficult to see because of the sunlight beaming in through the windows. I closed two shades.

And so Allen Ginsberg read his poem to us via YouTube. I will always remember standing among the seniors in this class sitting in desks grouped for the presentations, listening to his airy, conversational voice. Standing the farthest away in the back of the room, I had everyone in my field of view. I need to say that the classes' body language did not signal any problems. In fact, as you might imagine, the class listened in rapt attention.

In about two minutes, Ginsberg finished the poem.

And the narrator's recounting of his homosexual desire was open and graphic.

The room was quiet. The poem had had an effect. That much was clear. The question remained, and I asked again, "What do you make of the poem's language? No one answered at first. I waited. Gave some additional time to process, think. "Does it remind you of anything?"

Kaylee offered, "It reminds me of *Fifty Shades of Grey*," with a bit of a chuckle, I recall. And discussion began.

What do we know about the era? Were men and women openly talking about sexual desire? "No, of course not," I heard a student respond. "Why not?" I asked. "We hear a lot of expression of this desire today in many forms. Certainly it didn't hold true in the '50's and early '60's, despite the emerging expression in the Blues and Rock 'n' Roll. Most importantly here, we know that gay people could not be open and honest about their identity, much less, express such feelings of any desire. People holding cultural and institutional power would not allow that."

Kaylee smartly added that women were also subject to the oppression of expression of their own desires. She went on saying that for men the opposite was true. That men generally could use that language informally (what would become known the next year in the Presidential election, as "locker room talk"). She reminded us of the cultural revolution in gendered roles during the era—and its necessity for free and open conversation in our democracy.

After a pause, one student asked, who is the narrator? Is it a male or female?" We followed the pronouns as they progressed in the poem and looked to determine both the narrator and the audience. A student pointed to the phrase "like a girl," and we discussed the implications of that phrase, which included the important question, "What assumptions about gender identity are readers bringing to the poem to make that determination?" Another student asked if the phrase "like a girl" was sexist or if it was direct.

Kaylee, who made the connection to "Fifty Shades of Grey," returned to the connection and offered an insight into both the harsh language of the poem and the assumptions behind desire. Her stunning insight reflected an important point about the use of language to challenge common assumptions about a person's ability to break free and make one's own decisions about desire. A sticky wicket, for sure.

At this point I offered a question about the poem's narrator by looking at the anaphora. The repetition of "Please Master," beginning in the title itself, drew attention to itself. In fact, the repetition produced a certain irony, for why would one have to continue to ask the question? "Does the repetition construct an ironic narrator?" I asked. More, I added that the phrase "Please Master" might operate ironically, for the word "master" means a skilled practitioner at an art of skill but it also can mean an owner of servants or slaves. The contradiction, on the one hand, suggests a reverence for someone skilled, but on the other, it suggests a forced servitude. I leaned toward the later, for "we know of Allen Ginsberg challenging of authorities during his time, so in my reading that likely constructs his narrator as ironic."

Archer added of their work, their study of "Howl." They added this poem of Ginsberg's addressed the hypocrisy of the body public as injustice unfolded around the rights of African Americans, women, and people victimized by a deep-seated materialism and government penchant for war-mongering. They briefly addressed the poem "Howl" as affecting dissent. Then, the bell rang. No more time. Twelve minutes were up.

I congratulated the students for their work in our inquiry into poetic language, and the low-murmuring class gathered their gear to go. The day's presenters left their presentation preparation materials on my desk before they left. I approached that desk, too, and congratulated Steven for "hanging in there" with a difficult poem that challenged our sense for harsh language. and he replied, "Can't believe we heard it. That was amazing." We had just had a brief journey into language that challenged us all on multiple levels. Little did I know the cruelty that lie ahead because of a poem by Allen Ginsberg. After the reading and 12-minute discussion, students left class, and the language did float out into the hallways. It swirled into the howling currents of cruelty.

7 "Please Master," The Poem

Let's talk honestly about the poem, "Please Master" itself.

I have more to say to you about the aftermath following the reading of Allen Ginsberg's poem, "Please Master" in my senior class, but we need to have a conversation about this poem.

First, Please Master was not selected as a core work for the AP/ECE course. This point seems muddled from the start. The district never mentioned this fact, let alone emphasized it. Power chooses what power wants, and the absence of this fundamental point in public served as one means to silence the work of our classroom.

Frankly, I agree. This poem is not one that is or should be regularly included in high school literature curricula, even for the course I had designed. Ginsberg's major work "Howl" had been included as book of poetry for students to choose, as an entry point into our unit of inquiry, Voices from the Wilderness. Ginsberg is a major, American poet. His work is widely studied as important to American literature. I realize it's a little weird to quote a poetry organization in a letter and offer a footnote explaining that organization, but I think we need clarity about Allen Ginsberg as a major American figure during the Beat Generation. I quote the Poetry Foundation: 1

---

[1] The Poetry Foundation is a 501(c)(3) exempt private nonoperating foundation located in Chicago, Illinois. Established in 2003 upon receipt of a major gift from philanthropist Ruth Lilly, the Poetry Foundation evolved

"Allen Ginsberg was an acclaimed poet and a leading figure of the Beat Generation whose radical literary works and advocacy for social change left an indelible mark on American counterculture. Ginsberg first came to public attention in 1956 with the publication of *Howl and Other Poems* (City Lights Books)." I've been told by other scholars that Ginsberg's work had an enduring effect on the mid to late 1950's in ushering in language that would come to define the Beat Generation.

"Please Master's" language makes it a challenge, as it's immediately recognizable as containing "loaded language." The term "loaded language" as a literary term means especially value-laden language used rhetorically to appeal emotionally to an audience. In my own interpretation, the narrator has been long frustrated by a culture that rejects love between members of the same sex. The narrator clearly has a longing, but his frustrations are couched in language the narrator knows will not be accepted by a mainstream audience of his time period, just as he rejects the premise of the ritualized binary: male and female. He cannot accept the rejected framework and pleads. More, I interpret the narrator's loaded language as designed to connect him with his desired partner. Both know their relationship's illicit nature and its rejection based on their 1950's and '60's societal norms and habits. As we know, gay physical relationships were illegal in most all states in the United States during this time.

The repetition of the graphic sexual language rises to

---

from the Modern Poetry Association, which was a literary organization founded in 1941 to support the publication of *Poetry* magazine. The gift from Ruth Lilly allowed the Poetry Foundation to expand and enhance the presence of poetry in the United States and established an endowment that will fund *Poetry* in perpetuity.

a crescendo during the poem for obvious reasons, as it builds the argument for their connection on the page and builds a counterattack against the oppressive cultural practices that have silenced and rejected gay people, not only as legitimate democratic citizens but also as legitimate human beings. Clearly, there are others who disagree with my interpretation, and that's completely reasonable. I disagree, however, with those who call the work a pornographic anthem or any other term that suggests some kind of illegal obscenity. It's quite clear in my own thinking that Allen Ginsberg occupies a recognized and important role in American Letters, and to reduce a poem, published in a book of poems, The Fall of America, rests instead on the very same oppression that existed in the 1950's. Artists occupy a special place in culture, one that has been recognized by the Supreme Court of the United States.

In fact, Allen Ginsberg is an important literary figure whose work was the subject of a Supreme Court ruling, initially accused of obscenity, which presaged the counter-culture movement of the 1960's. In the tradition of Walt Whitman, however, Ginsberg focuses on human experience, and sings its multitudes.

However, the language of the poem makes it unlikely to succeed in a general studies high school classroom, even when the course is sanctioned by a regulating university. That much I understand and agree with the district and my colleagues at South Windsor High School, who were at least uncomfortable with the language, with even some of my colleagues downright upset by it. I understand. I acknowledged as much to them and the district. To disagree, however, is in the nature of a democratic society, and to disregard disagreement is to reject educational and democratic principles. So, I still felt a teachable moment at hand at the end of a unit when a senior pressed his intellectual curiosity to a classmates' presentation of educational, literary inquiry.

We would fall into the same hijacking context by lingering over my interpretation of the graphic language in what the College Board calls a "close reading." Ginsberg's narrator uses graphic language to depict a homosexual sexual act, so it's not productive to deal with it in ways that ignore poetry. If you want to read it, the choice is yours; if you don't want to read, the choice is yours. The point is, we will not do that here. On this page.

We will not fall prey to the prurient claims and desire of some to focus entirely on sexualized language, and I reject imposing that framework on our conversation. That premise remains a central reason for the silence that almost fatally stalled our conversations about reading, writing, and learning to begin.

We didn't fall prey to any such urge during the class when the poem was read. In fact, in the Department of Children and Families' report, mandated by the laws of Connecticut, when a school district refers an adult, the case was promptly closed after finding no substantiated claims. Instead, it noted students generally reported that the conversation about the poem, although highly unusual, was discussed in academic terms.

You likely haven't been told this, but a group of Allen Ginsberg scholars wrote to our Board of Education and superintendent in defense of Ginsberg's work—soon after the shockingly fast attempt to terminate me as your teacher. They weren't the only ones. Ironic. Many wrote. None were heard beyond the closed door of the administrative building. Some wrote about Allen Ginsberg's poem "Please Master" as a holy expression of love within the confines of a society that did not recognize and even rejected love between two men. Steve Silverman, author and former teaching assistant of Allen Ginsberg, wrote a moving tribute to the historically-based and artistic structure and movement of the poem as a rising crescendo of religious magnitude as a form and an expression of love. I thought it a smartly ironic swipe at those who insist on applying a religious framework to a literary work. What's important here are the voices of support for art, and it's a motivation for me in reaching out to you in this letter. The environment of the days and months following the reading, again, left no room for conversation such as this.

Others wrote and addressed your classmates' intellectual curiosity. Helen Vendler, the renowned poetry critic from Harvard—look these people up! They are as real as the words you are reading now—named Steven's intellectual inquiry as among the highest of scholarship. The stuff of intellectual excellence rests on curiosity driving us deeper into an area under study, and to share that thinking.

That's just incredible, isn't it? Turns out the poem we heard is situated within a set of poetic traditions, known to readers and scholars; second, your colleague represents the finest learner according to a Harvard University scholar professor. To engage in conversation about language by raising questions connected to our ongoing conversations about poetry was of the highest order. I remain in awe of this student who lived the AP/ECE academic goal to "enter the conversation." It makes me dance to write about him to you as an honestly- and intellectually-driven mind; and, third, none of this was part of any conversation I'm blown away that these perspectives that did not get air to breathe. This is why I write to you. Not to get back into the poem itself so much as to try to have a conversation that was scuttled.

You know, I've gone over this in my head and in conversations with people close to me over and over. Let me share with you a statement from the Advanced Placement course description, which announced the content and language to be expected by students taking this course across the country:

> In an ongoing effort to recognize the widening cultural horizons of literary works written in English, the AP English Literature Development Committee will consider and include diverse authors in the respective reading list. Issues that might, from a specific cultural viewpoint, raise controversy, including references to ethnicities, nationalities, religions, races, dialects, gender, or class, are often represented artistically in works of literature. The Development Committee is committed to careful review of such potentially controversial material. Still, recognizing the universal value of literary art that probes difficult and harsh life experiences and so deepens understanding, the committee emphasizes that fair representation of issues and people may occasionally include controversial material. Since AP students have chosen a program that directly involves them in college-level work, the AP English Literature and Composition Exam depends on a level of maturity consistent with the age of 12th-grade students who have engaged in thoughtful analysis of literary texts. But that's not what I want to say. See what I mean? Even the language that seeks to be true and honest can fail. I'm not writing to cast blame—and that gets in the way all the time in our lives.

College Board

I'm glad for students to have "chosen a program that involve[d] them in college-level work." And while I'd been trained on and learned much of this challenging content of courses such as this, which explores some of the most consequential literature of the English-speaking people from over two-thousand years, it's clear that it was widely ignored. As a result, I hope to draw to your attention that "in an ongoing effort to recognize the widening cultural horizons of literary works written in English, the AP English Literature Development Committee will consider and include diverse authors in the respective reading list. Issues that might, from a specific cultural viewpoint, raise controversy, including references to ethnicities, nationalities, religions, races, dialects, gender, or class, are often represented artistically in works of literature." I notice the word "often," as great works are often our perspective-shakers, and an integrity of inquiry seeks those moments out instead of turning them away, as my last superintendent seemed to suggest we must.

Now, I'm thinking about the woods, about growing up in an America that pulls up certain plants by their roots to maintain a homogeneity that does not exist. I'd rather, though, write about the beauty of each of my eighty-eight students, because of their unique identities. I'm thinking about the pain of rejection and the attempt to find one's place. I'm thinking about learning as a larger communal act of gratitude for each other. We can find ways to be grateful for the act of inquiry itself, without having to rely on any gendered, racialized, ethnicized, religious-ized—or any other -ized categories. That's the promise of the 14th Amendment. Just let people be themselves.

94

I just mean to say that thoughtful readers should bring their own interpretations to the world, raising questions, without the judgement and rejections of the so called "properness" of that language and those interpretations. I am always open to that conversation. We should avoid the temptation to leave the world of reading, writing, teaching, and learning to impositions of judgements of character about educators (readers) who believe in learning. To land an albatross on an educational mast is to cease movement. This distinction between interpretation of literature and assertions against character has hidden in that black hole, stifling conversation about learning, and teaching and the integrity of inquiry. Until now. Let's keep talking openly.

So, when my student brought a poem to class during the closing twelve minutes of our 75-minute class period, little did I realize that the same authorities challenged by art in the 1950's would also rear in the 21st century. I have learned to embrace multiple perspectives, without placing moral judgments upon readers during my educational career, and I am still open, despite the controversial nature of it.

...

As I continue to write and revise this letter, now in 2025, my reading of the poem shifts. Grows. Rereading the poem again for this letter, I now notice the language itself speaks to the silences we grapple with here, in this letter. In other words, the poet casts this absolute sound-barrier-braking language into the silence of bias and prejudice to fill the gap with bold rebellion. Every writer makes language choices, just I have made here with you. Ginsberg, I have learned had had a longstanding, off and on relationship with Neal Cassidy, the subject of the poem. Not just the subject of the narrator's desire but also an important figure the Beat Generation. Apparently, he was an excellent driver, so Ken Kesey got him to take over the Further Bus for much of their famous trip across America, having crazy parties, including LSD, and generally rejecting "The Establishment." For which Ken Kesey was famous, and for which Thomas Wolfe's *The Kool-Aid Acid Test* helped give voice.

These writers did not give into the cruel silences imposed by hypocritical American mainstream culture but filled them with language and stories, and poetry. I will not give in to the cruelty of silence but fill it with the story of a confidence in inquiry in class that day, February 25, 2015.

Those voices had been hijacked. There was no discussion with you, the community, to talk not just about these points of view but also anything else about that fateful day in February of 2015. I wonder if these words that have been under the blanket of silence but are now in my letter to you will be seen? Heard? It's important to make visible the joy this letter embraces under the conditions that rejected them. Some reading my letter to you may have held and even still hold the very points of view that would maintain the silence. I still embrace those different viewpoints. Even now. I write to you, though, with the warmth of conviction for the passion and joy for language and learning that did not underscore those perspectives. I hope you hold tightly the joy of discovery of all kinds of ideas important to you during your life.

The weight of this silence lifts as I write. Yes, it has been cruel, not just to me, not just to you, but also to the underlying sense of community trust in learning. And for that, I've been furious—but I will not carry myself furious. Not the way I will carry myself. I will not engage in slander of character. No not in that way. I'll write to you with an honest voice that addressees an issue essential to our democratic life, so that we can talk on this page.

I am now writing to you to about the value of taking a stance of inquiry in your lives. Many forces are not only influencing teachers as they select books and design units of study but also affecting our own conversations with family and friends. Although there's never a black and white answer about speaking or not speaking, we must avoid today's pressures to avoid talking, because it may unintentionally offend another person or group.

No, I'm not bothered by the poem or its language; rather, I'm still bothered by the fact that we haven't talked about it. May this letter help pierce that silence.

8 THE DAYS AFTER FEBRUARY 25, 2015

I remember writing an early draft as I attempted to capture a morning in my teaching life after I had first learned the district would seek my termination and remove me from our classroom:

4:29 am: February 27, 2015

Morning Ritual

During the digital moment when the clock's green numbers blur from 4:29 to 4:30 and that alarm blasts, I am vaguely aware of the conscious world. Still, I am thinking about my high school students. As millions of teachers ritually do, I'm thinking about my students and their classes. I turn the hot and cold faucets to prepare a shower. I will step in and let the water bead down over me. Like the warm water cascading from the shower head, my work pours over me, and I tip my chin upwards to fully accept it.

As semiconsciousness turns to consciousness in the shower, like an unopened gift, my teaching brain animates. It jumps into its own conversation. The muted narrative roils in my

mind. *great discussion yesterday about laws and morality. but would kyle work with well rachel after yesterday's conversation about eye contact? how to support her—avoid large group questions to her. how would georgia feel after the special education meeting yesterday and the conflict with her mom; group them; sit with them and support them to begin class...* I hop out. Dry. And start to dress. The green light on the clock glows 4:29. The early narrative continues in my mind. *laptop carts. need to sign out the laptop cart for periods 6 and 7 on friday. make copies this afternoon for thursday's period 5 class: reflection on close reading activity after reading thoreau's "on civil disobedience" should consider their own collaborative role in their small groups, their new understanding of using multiple word meanings. connected, patterned ideas to shape an idea. what does it mean to them to be independent? after the experience in groups? —encourage connection to class walk in woods last week. journaling, and then writing metaphors about experience while reading selections from henry david thoreau's walden (remember: type up that handout later this morning...also, with Francis, have conversation about the content of reflection for our shared class: ask for her thoughts about range of reflective questions. add? delete? or*

otherwise revise?). I feel for her, as our principal gives her –
a new teacher-- a lot of grief, especially for her dress…i
can't believe he confronted her about a small tattoo under
her sleeve…she works her tail off for her kids… **The digital**
green numbers slowly blur, changing from :29 to :30.
remember: enter grades for denotative meaning quiz for
period 2. more, share results with and group ronnie and jake
with mattie and clarissa for the next day's extension lesson.
ronnie and jake are still struggling with the concept, so
mattie and clarissa can exercise help those two break
through the fog. confidence! you can rock the world! oh,
call deion's mom, this afternoon, to update her. he was
amazing yesterday! gave earnest appreciation for heather's
work when we closed class. now that's learning! check in
today, too, about next week's department meeting and short
presentation Dave asked me to give on AP strategies…apply
to grades nine and ten—remember, trying to embed
sequenced skill sets and affective understandings earlier to
prompt additional, capable students to consider and succeed
with our AP courses…whoa. hold up. question. are we
pushing young scholars without addressing habit of mind?—
the attitude and mind-set necessary to think of ap courses as
a place of challenging and independent scholarship?
connection to uconn scholarship?

Then, I notice the digital green reads, in a snap, 4:30. It feels as if the world ramps up even before the alarm sound bleats, and my thoughts churn like a subterranean river, now, in my role as chair for the Commission on Instruction and Professional Development for the Connecticut Education Association. *reach out to jeanette. ask for agenda input. need to discuss an approach to engage teachers in connecticut in conversation about the core proficiencies for new district, professional development committees. recent legislative changes. implications. new statues. help all students. improve learning...*then, in the fraction of that moment, the alarm goes off. It's 4:30 am.

4:30 am

Conscious Ritual

Wednesday would have given birth to mid-week possibility, and, as every morning when I get up at 4:30 am, the cats are hungry. They trill and rub the bedroom door's threshold to cry their hunger and morning affections. I get up, walk down the hall, and descend the stairs, turning the lights on to lead the way. The cats follow, fleet of foot, darting in and out; we enter our wood-floored kitchen. I feed both and the dog, giving all fresh water. I pull the coffee from the freezer, ladle six scoops into the percolator basket. I make coffee.

Then, as millions of teachers do in the first years of the 21st century to start their day, I would sit down, log in, and prepare for the day. I would prepare to meet each student from their own life experience, cultural knowledge, and learning style, to empower each student's independence—or at least I would try. So, I would track from the kitchen into our family room, colored by muted earth tones of green and yellow. Framed pictures of my wife, my two children, my brothers, my parents, my wife's parents, nestled within rows of books on the shelves, watch over me as I nestle in. On my couch, I would open my laptop, browser, and navigate to *The Onion* and read the link to *The New York Times*, and dive deeper into an article of consequence for my work. I might skim a short opinion piece by Kathleen Parker in *The Washington Post* about social media, where she wonders about Twitter's role as America's conscience; I also might bump into a short piece about Scott Walker, who has instituted sweeping attacks against teacher protections; and, then linger over a piece about a woman wearing a hijab to a job interview with Abercrombie and Fitch. The Supreme

Court will hear her case. Also, the Court will hear a case on gay marriage. I would have thought to myself that the latter two pieces especially would help in our upcoming unit, Listening to Voices on the Lower Frequency, in my sophomore American Literature course. So, I would add the articles to my Diigo library for later reference.

Next, I'd open a new tab, navigate to and log into the district's computer-lab/laptop calendar, check for availability, and secure laptops for Friday's Period 6 and 7 class, when I would wheel the cart to my room, 147, from the department office during the five-minute passing time, hoping the cart would have been returned in time after its last busy use. I would refill my coffee, stirring in more clover honey from the Hurst Family Farm in Hebron. I do like it sweet, and the clover honey would help with spring allergies. After, I'd draft reflection questions for Period 5, saving the draft in a folder on my MacBook for my colleague to review and comment on.

They'd look something like this:

Sophomore American Literature   Name:

Mr. Olio   Period:

Learner Reflection Following "Civil Disobedience" Discussion

1. List one key sentence your group discussed:

2. Idea about civil disobedience that Thoreau's sentence seems to express, now that you have had a conversation (no need for consensus here):

3. How does it <u>sequence</u> with a sentence before or after it? How does the idea develop or otherwise grow, as a result?

4. List a word choice in the sentence that deepens an idea about civil disobedience that Thoreau advances:

Discussion/Collaboration Reflection

5. How is this word choice powerful? Connotation? Denotation? Figure of speech? What make the language seem so important?

6. Summarize the coolest comment about civil disobedience from _____:

7. Why this is important to your learning about civil disobedience?

8. Appreciation about the role a specific student filled in the group discussion. Make sure to name someone specifically!

Next, I enter Period 2 quiz grades, and I zip off an email to Jeanette with an agenda draft, with questions, for the upcoming commission meeting next week. Our cat hops up onto the couch, looking for attention, snuggling alongside me. He saps me out of my thought about the commission meeting.

Instead I put the laptop aside for a few minutes. I paused this writing. I stop the story. Here. Now. For you in this letter.

Likely, I would have re-read the passages from *The Adventures of Huckleberry Finn* and finished working on the document I would have begun to modify to assist my two college preparatory sophomore classes in their reading. I would group students who would talk about passages from *The Adventures of Huckleberry Finn* and "Civil Disobedience" for Periods 2 and 5. Erasing, crossing out, moving, considering combinations the students have asked for. I would decide their groups for the day. I would settle on grouping Kyle, Rachel, and Georgia in Period 2 to offer extra support given their recent personal and learning experiences.

Once settled on the groups, I would have taken out

notecards, folding them length-wise into table tents and, on the one side, writing the four names for each group, and, on the other, writing notes of encouragement, such as, "Welcome to class!" and "Glad you're here!" Students would know to find their groups when they come to our classroom by finding their welcome cards on their desks. In their groups, students would have reviewed their *Huck Finn* characterization poster and made connections from "Civil Disobedience" for a class gallery walk. Each group would have presented a different moment in Huck's journey to contend with his society's incomprehensible treatment of others, especially of Jim, Miss Watson's slave.

Finished, I would have gathered my gear and leapt into the car to head off for school. I wouldn't have headed off to school because of the common belief that teachers have to educate ALL students but because I'm ALL in. A teacher's entire identity. The very definition of self-wrapped in commitment to freedom of thought. I never once went to school because I had to but because I loved to learn. The confidence I hold in learning is so palpable, that I could feel it streaming over my head as I would stand in the shower every morning getting ready; could feel it cascading over my face; could feel it beading over your entire body as it falls to the floor. I have always felt that reading and writing offered keys to the kingdom of our country, and all around me seemed to agree. Some say that teaching is some underground activity, but I was always above ground, in the light. In fact, being honest about the world can help wash the ignorance that causes misunderstanding and strife. Some have characterized this as ingénue; perhaps, but that view ignores a full commitment that all students are capable. Are worthy. And, that we need to pour faith into you and your capacity to learn, capacity to teach know, capacity to engage. I've always believed in students. I've always believed in the merit of ideas and necessity of their exchange. I always thought there was an agreement that a public education was essential to a healthy democracy, and I gladly accepted that covenant.

Instead, I would glance at the world clock on the shelf: it would have read 11:30 am in Paris, France; but, in Hebron, Connecticut it was 5:30 a.m.

I would gather the cat next to me and mourn. I would not go to school to teach today.

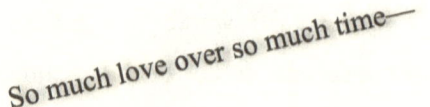

So much love over so much time—

. . .

At the time I wrote this, I had hoped to share a crafted moment of my teaching-life ritual, design a page-image. I had hoped it would serve to fill in the silences created by hackneyed images of the toiling English teacher, bent over papers for a lifetime, tied to a desk. For sure, teachers devote themselves and spend a ton of time on their students' work and the texts they read. So here, in my letter to you, I bring that image back. Now. I like it. It feels expressive of an attention that I held over my thirty years. Each teacher's unique—so, too, each teacher's crafted image. I'm happy to share this one specially for you.

I was thinking ten years ago to explain a morning of everyday drive to create exceptional experiences for you, giving a glimpse of the devotion that develops from the attention to each of you. I had hoped to share a real teaching morning. Instead, now, as I write to you, I also understand that this vignette has sat in my computer for over nine years as a series of paragraphs, that lacked a crafting of a deeper context. A sad tale about loss that had not been spoken or written.

The very essence of possibility is that risk of sinking to the bottom of the sea into the cold. Who knows how far down we can dive if we develop habits of examining feelings, ideas, and experiences. The bottom of the ocean is cold and dark, so possibility requires risk.

Silence is a kind of dead zone, and at least the ocean has life at its enormously cold depths. After our 12-minutes-before-cruelty, the poem-turned-prurient gossip buzzed in the public's ears covered all other conversation in silence. I write the tale to you in this letter of a recollection that now feels lost and foreign. I don't feel the confusion or anger. I dive again in this letter, like I had done as a teacher. What had been a twenty-three-year abiding pursuit of excellence, disappeared, leaving not even a lump for me or you, the audience, to remember. To be recovered. Yet, as the power of words and our ability to use them honestly builds, I see that I have found and built a new life, filled with the joy that still roils within me. I miss the mornings of assembling material for students in retirement from the classroom, but find solace in placing these words, one by one, together, to say to you that our building is never done.

I write to you now, then. My awareness in the world continues. My trust in inquiry remains. I'm not sure exactly how it happens, but it wraps its warmth around me each time I open my eyes in the morning. I wonder if it drives me to the page and I continue to write, or if the writing is what helps continue the joy, to seek a way for us to talk. No, I will not give up. This epistolary form allows me space for a personal voice. It's been a long time coming. I urge myself to work the words to move out of their hiding. My own joy, I have discovered, cannot fade, if I can use this opportunity to write to you.

9 OUR GANG OF LEARNERS

Writing to you now, ten years later, I am reminded our voices can emerge from the chaos of injustice to share experience we value. So much of our world is changing, but, at the same time, so little has changed. Our ways of thinking about our contradictory world is always in flux, so my letter can reignite our past conversation that matters for each and every one of you now. I ask, then, what do you need to say about learning? How are you feeling about public conversations about issues important to you? To your community? To public education? To the freedom to read? To our democracy? Your community spends a lot of money and effort to support a public education system, allegedly designed for student learning, so what do you expect from it? What do you want for the family you may be imagining? For the people in your community? For your nation? If we want places that nurture the human spirit of inquiry; if we want places that make possible a lifetime of personal growth; if we want experiences to empower younger people to gain the skills and habits of minds necessary to care for themselves and shape healthy communities; if we want to ensure democratic practices thrive to maintain a country of freedom, we should ask our schools to embrace and to forward authentic inquires in learning.

The thinking that school is really only supposed to get one a "good job" stems from a past that no longer exists. You've heard the research that indicates many of your future jobs still have yet to be created. What about using inquiry as a means to think well, to use reading and writing and collaboration as tools for problem-solving and creation, creating a life for one's self, whether that means working for another or creating your own business. I observe that some get trapped into a singular way of thinking, where a single answer exists, but to support yourselves in the twenty-first century of technological upheaval and change, singular thinking just won't keep you afloat. I'm sure you know this, but I'm asking how you see that playing out in our education system—and how it will continue to play out in your life. I believe districts will need to fully put the industrial model of authority, backed primarily by control and designed for singular results into the past. Ironically, Ralph Waldo Emerson noted, "A foolish consistency is the hobgoblin of little minds."

If the turn-of-the-millennium warning that most students' jobs will not have been created while they're still in K-12 school, what are the implications for learning? I believe if students learn to ask questions, explore new ways of thinking, and create new ways of solving problems, then whether they want to work for someone else, create a new business, create music, create art, or write and engage the world with a sense of wonder and joy, then we need a footing of inquiry and creation. Shutting down inquiry for the sake of maintaining a status quo of control over students, maintaining legacies of biases, recreates a world that no longer exists. A paradox, eh? Make no mistake, to forward a set of religious values, cultural values, or personal values that restricts inquiry destroys the very idea of American ingenuity and sense of possibility. An undercurrent of bias flows counter to a surface current of inquiry and ingenuity that will only broil the waters.

I shift my voice in my letter, then, to a voice of advocacy. I hope you hear the marker I leave for you. We will always confront headwinds and undercurrents that make it tough to be yourself. In a world always telling you who to be and how to be it, I hope you remember from our classes to question everything. As I write to you now in 2025, my sixty-year-old self recognizes and celebrates your twenty-something lives in progress. I'm so glad to dance with you on this page with words of confidence and possibility for each of you. Each deserve the freedom to inquire, explore, and then make choices, even though we know that the world around us boxes us into its vision for us. More, let me extend our conversation: every student deserves the tools to think for themselves and not simply regurgitate past virtues and vices. That's a central challenge with AI—we must embrace the value of inquiry to avoid forwarding past prejudice; a deft set of inquiry skills may help us reject the myth that AI *knows* best.

All of our lives will change, shift, and morph. You know this. And we're still searching, seeking, inquiring, and hopefully participating in the unfurling. And our lives will continue to unfold. To me, that's the green light at the end of Daisy's dock that Fitzgerald created at the end of the novel *The Great Gatsby*. The end! But it's not! It never ends. If we're inquiring and creating, we're alive. Our human spirit is alive. Our lives are always in progress, in this way.

I hope you clearly see what's at stake and why I've been compelled to write to you. You are constantly changing and growing. It's more than ever the stuff of your generation, so I write to advocate that you embrace the open waters. Others will choose ticky-tacky answers, stagnation, and censorship. Others will place a set of black-and-white answers in the front of the room with students in proverbial rows and ignore most every other possibility. In fact, as I discovered growing up and after February 25, 2015, many of those possibilities will be labeled as "evil" or "prurient" or in some way "undermining," when in fact the opposite is true. Inquiry is the marrow of discovery. And I am happy to write to you that I know a gang of you for certain who are living this!

Introducing The Gang

So, I leap with joy off the tip of a wave as one of you makes your way into the lights of New York City, literally shining beams of theater lights on the stages of Broadway. Another of you pilots planes for an airline in the northwestern most region of Alaska, following his dream to pilot planes through the sky. Another engineers sonic production with a collaborative team making movies in Atlanta, a new mecca for American films. Yet another of you produces UX content for an engineering company right here in Connecticut, a guitar aficionado and writer. Still another of you guides communities of faith in the province of Quebec, situated in Montreal. Of course, our hero, the Eagle Scout is about to begin his family by marrying his fiancée, while writing, creating, and publishing his own music, caring for animals, and dabbling with the FBI and systems of package delivery. I write about each one of these former students in present tense as they each dance with each moment:

Archer, Michael, Kaylee, Hayle, Sarah, and Steven.

These amazing former students—each from my AP/ECE class in 2015—have put their inquiries to practical use in the world. The Gang. As you may remember, during all of our work together in class ten years ago, whether as sophomores or seniors, when drawing from each other's thinking and writing, engaging new perspectives, and making something of them yourselves, writers and thinkers need to attribute—or acknowledge those key voices we draw ideas from. In fact, we need permission to use other's words—especially their roles in stories such as this. So, this part of my letter and conversation with you has permission from The Gang. I hope the homage is evident in their naming in this memoir. These are the students who hung tight with me against the attack on art, gender identity, learning, and democratic conversation.

If I could, I would name each and every eighty-six of you—and ask what each has gone on to do with your lives so far: my last students at South Windsor High School in the spring of 2015, but I cannot. The circumstances following February 25, 2015 interrupted our underlying lines of communication. So, I write this letter to reach out, forging open avenues with the written word. I'm especially inspired to do so by Archer, Kaylee, Hayle, Michael, Sarah, and Steven.

The Gang, comprising six heroic students from that AP/ECE class, distinguished themselves as young adults and students during our work in 2014-2015. During the debacle, and just as importantly, in the years following, to this day. They were interested in ideas. They're still interested in ideas. They were interested in the arts. They're still interested in the arts. They cared about their high school community. They care about their communities now.

These students cared so much about the literary arts, they physically showed up just about ten years ago at the Board of Education meeting on March 5, 2015. Of course, you may remember in my earlier telling that I wasn't there. I was at a friend's house in South Windsor. I was not allowed to attend.

I remember having to watch a Board of Education meeting from a friend's house in South Windsor, who had the local cable channel broadcasting but who went to the meeting to offer words of support.

It felt like I was watching my own funeral.

People spoke of me in past tense verbs. It felt like an obituary, so it's emotionally difficult to write to you about it even now. To think about the death of a career. To think about the passing of an identity. The language of kindness and care are models for all of us.

The Gang showed. And they showed care. Their courage ten years ago is worth a film. Certainly, their stories are worth my gratitude. You can imagine. You can feel. You can grasp the risk Archer, Steve, Michael, Hayle, Sarah, and Kaylee faced by standing up in a public meeting. You know, as I write to you, that moment rises as one of the outcries that pierced the public silence, and for this I am blown away. It reminds me so much of the capacity to challenge and to offer multiple points of view—to not be silenced by one authoritative perspective upheld by its institutional authority. The Gang assembled in support for the first time in a public space, in response to the developing injustice shoveled out by the district.

Now, they had role models that night. Two other former students, one who graduated in 2000 and another in 2002, I think, began the public comments portion of the meeting. They brought their public voices in support of art, integrity in questioning, deep and meaningful learning, and the celebration of each human spirit in their own, unique form.

When they began that Board of Education open forum segment, each spoke about their intellectual and personal growth as a result of an open, questioning, supporting and affirming education. They both pointed to me, and they both acknowledged my contributions to their community of learning. The two spoke eloquently about the ongoing challenges students face to grow up in a world that rejects the voices of artists and their work based on personal biases; they reminded the Board that they had specific experiences in my class that helped them learn to navigate the world's challenges—and to solve problems through engagement. In fact, echoing their words here in summary reminds me of the power of an education based in open conversation, honesty, and integrity in intellectual inquiry.

More, their words emphasized to me that we all should be learning from you—my former and current students. For example, not only did one of my former students teach me new language, characterizing that long-ago injustice circumstance as a "broglio" in an interview with a David Freedlander, a national journalist for the *Daily Beast* but also she put into words a world she thought important to build that her fellow citizens deserved. She spoke to the Board of Education about embracing, not censoring, the literary arts. I agree, a world without embracing a full-throated support of English Language Arts risks a banal existence—lacking in vitality, originality, and discovery of what makes us human. More, another former student, beautifully articulated, as an experienced college administrator, the life-saving moments an education can offer, especially for those who have experienced traumas growing up. Their own work in universities over the years has engaged students from the entire human spectrum. Both students served as model democratic denizens that night. I hope you were able to hear these former students speak.

Kaylee's mother had written a compelling article the week before the Board meeting in defense of her daughter's English teacher, piercing the fraught silence. She spoke at the Board with the six students from the AP/ECE class siting in the audience, along with a few of their parents, in support, too. Her words would also help to rescue me from my own drowning.

It would take another several months, though, to open conversation with The Gang after that Board meeting. Because a member at our church had been friends with Steven's mom, we initially overheard each other's whispers standing behind the pews after services. I was able to learn that he was surviving the ordeal, and he was able to learn through this channel of my burning desire to know whether he was okay. I hadn't known how Steven was being supported during the heartbreaking silence that blanketed us. I didn't know whether he may have felt as if he had some antagonistic role in this 4th act of tragedy. I didn't know how he felt, and that really was hard to deal with period. I could only imagine his impossible experience, because of my own. I was crestfallen over the possibility harm could come to him in some way. That a poem in an English classroom had created conditions of harm for him in the public sphere. Given the threat—and under extreme emotional stress, I feared for his circumstance, as well.

I'm sure you don't know this: the day after they took my badge and keys from me and sent me home, I was watched by a car out front our house for several days. It would linger for an hour and then leave. Then it would return, repeating a pattern. I'm not sure why I was so afraid in that moment, but it made me feel uncomfortable to speak to just about anyone. It had turned into an ugliness that scared the hell out of me. The consequences had begun to seem insanely dangerous. So, to connect initially in some small way with Steven through his mother and to find out he didn't carry feelings of responsibility, was more than some small relief.

Our hero's story is incredible: One of The Gang.

I remember the day we all eventually met. That first lunch felt like the back sliding door opening up for the first time after winter on a warm spring day. I felt summer air again. And seeing each smiling face, sharing coffee together, and then sitting out in the grass outside the restaurant gave us back the connection that had been taken away. They named themselves, The Gang, as we talked about our experiences during the class and after. We remembered going to a comedy skit Archer had presented with other students in the library one night. We moved on to some of the other funny stories, like having to sneak out early from seeing Shakespeare's *Hamlet* on stage at Hartford Stage because of a bus conflict for our ride home. We laughed, too, about Sarah's prize-winning essay, after she had entered an essay from class into a writing contest and won. We laughed that it earned a B+ in class. That first project resulted from our first inquiry in our senior AP/ECE class, dealt with what's called a genre of writing call a pastiche essay—an unusual form of writing. Like the term "pastiche," the writer connects seemingly disconnected scenes relying on forms, images, and repetition and other means of transition. The ordering matters.

We had read "Our Secret," a stunning pastiche essay, where the writer Susan Griffin braids forms of journalism, personal essay, and history to weave seemingly disconnected images of Nazi Germany, rocketry, and familial relations to explore the silences wrought by a lack of responsible reflection on our past. Our silence. A powerful essay, it brought a myriad of new forms into the conversation about writing for students in ways that broke old modes of five-paragraph-essay thinking, establishing creative spaces for new thinking for the year. To explore, discover, and create new ideas with language is to dance like a wave of the sea.

The conversation flowed again. Learning our relationships were intact and knowing a sense of goodness survived, I took a deep breath and exhaled. To try to rebuild our capacity for conversation that had been more than interrupted—crushed, was to plug back into an ethernet of cracking connection. The district's gag orders directing me to avoid any contact with students ended with their graduation, and our relationship survived. I could breathe more knowing The Gang had not fallen into the black hole.

The Gang countered cruelty with a sense of losing something even more than an English teacher. How and why would the district treat an educator with such public disdain when that educator had literally devoted twenty years of his life to students and families in the district. Kaylee noted, "Almost every student in this school has heard far worse in and around school—and certainly outside of school—and never had the chance to ask questions, talk openly, and think honestly about any of it." She's right. For sure, our intent did not include a search for the salacious. What's the purpose of that? There are important habits of learning at stake. There's the very act of asking questions; the very conversations we have; and the sharing of community of people with whom we live. The students agreed.

I remember asking Steven that summer if he thought it was a good idea to conduct an interview to capture his thinking about the events. So, at the South Windsor Public Library, about two months after graduation, we sat down. I first wanted to make sure he was okay and then to understand his perspective—so I listened to him talk about learning— about his development as a person and student over his life.

He spoke with a smile growing on the corners of lips about the Scouts. He had been a hands-on learner, one who also thrived outside. As part of his story about scouting and curiosity, about serving and creating connections with the community, he told me about the bench he had made for the town as part of his Eagle badge. It's very difficult to imagine a student of mine, with such curiosity and interest in the world, would have to contend with the cruelty that bloomed like a black rose. That's what heroes do, though. They cut paths in new territories. Given notions of taboo, this student had sunk his teeth into the course—and I admire him for it.

Let me finish this move, drawing further attention to The Gang's advocacy out from the hole of silence that has made it so difficult for us to talk. I hope you're hearing as much as I think I'm saying—and I hope the words of this letter fill in the silence of the past with stories about your own fellow students who have continued to dance with the world. These South Windsor Public School students attended and stood for themselves and their vision of the world. More, I hope they push you to think about those people who can help you open conversation in your own life, especially using your reading, writing, and thinking skills. I believe in the very human right of learning and growing; it invites us to the center of our lives, if we press on it.

So search. Write about it. Share it.

I'm sure each of you, as I write, can think about a time when you played the role of hero as a learner. Whether that had been supporting a classmate who was depressed; contributing to a club or team to which you belonged; or, digging into an issue needing a solution. We all face challenges, some more difficult and seemingly insurmountable than others.

At the beginning of this letter to you, I frankly didn't know how I would tackle all the feelings of confusion, hurt, appreciation, and joy. I occupied a weird space. Trashed by the school district that heaped hell on me. I imagine you remember the public beating the district gave me. In fact, the assistant superintendent had written a report filled with challengeable allegations and also released my termination letter, which *The Hartford Courant* got their hands on through an FOI request and posted it with little if any context. I'll never forget seeing it in the paper. It added to the black hole of impenetrability that I hope this letter seeks to unpack. The Gang has been instrumental. I thank you.

...

In fact, It's not possible to list all those people who wrote on behalf of the teaching and service to the community of South Windsor. Scores of people did write letters of support. Several even wrote and were published in the local newspaper.

As I write to you, I'm struck by the power of letters to record the history of a perspective. Letters such as this one lift a more personal tone than essays, but a problem arises from my personal point of view. It is mine. You each have your perspective about the course and the class that day—and

122

the days that have followed. So, it's important to be transparent and make my own words clear without dictating to you how you should feel about this event in our lives. The power wielded by words can be misconstrued, misused, and confused, if not causing downright harm. I've been leery about writing with power dynamics in play, and I hope I've pulled the curtain back to let you know I'm not playing tricks with you, regardless of your point of view. I've always respected my students. I respect you. I've always trusted students and believed in their capacity to think for themselves.

As I've gone through the drafts writing to you, I've reread the letters from (at the time) students, former students, South Windsor parents, parents of South Windsor students, colleagues, former colleagues, and members of my town and church, and one speaks to the idea of valuing learning. Please forgive me for quoting one in full here, but it's worth bringing to the conversation:

> Dear Members of South Windsor Board of Education:
>
> I present myself, an alumnus of the class of 2003, as a mind and person strongly shaped by the level of scholarship experienced in South Windsor Public Schools. I hold a master's degree from Boston University, as well as a Bachelor of Arts in History and a Bachelor of Arts in Music Education. I'm now employed in my seventh year as a teacher in another Connecticut district. As an alumnus, a current teacher, a citizen of the state of Connecticut, and former resident of South Windsor, I write out of concern for the course being set out by the South Windsor Public School's leadership in light of recent events.
>
> As an educator, I am very much aware of the responsibility of the school district, and thus the employees of the South Windsor Board of Education, to operate in

loco parentis, while also fostering classrooms that support students in realizing their full potential as self-actualized members of our community. I recognize that the response to recent events in South Windsor High School's AP English course has been undertaken in the light of these tenents yet a fear that in concern for the swift dealing with severe crackdown on this matter

The board is acting errantly, and not for the betterment of the school and town wide community of South Windsor. While the court of public opinion may be loud indeed and while some may vociferously call for the tremendous disciplinary action (i.e. the termination of David Olio's contract), let us listen to reason and ensure that any decision is made with discretion.

From my perspective on Mr. David Olio, I had the pleasure of experiencing his classroom in level 4 honors American literature as a sophomore in the academic year 2000 to 2001. The lessons learned in David's classroom were of incredible importance to me as a maturing young adult fostering critical thinking skills, gaining an awareness of perspective and bias extant in the written word—not to mention in my own assumptions and worldview —and by allowing for the exercise of empathy when interacting both with peers and literature. By my own estimation at the time, I thought him a very good teacher even if, or perhaps especially since, he held very high expectations of his students.

And reflecting on my experiences I recall that while studying the works of Emily Dickinson, he did not step in and dictate how poetry should be analyzed or interpreted, but rather support us students going forth and teasing out understanding ourselves. I remember stumbling in attempting to even follow the text—let alone the subtext—of the lines, "the poet searched village/ and when about to ring/ for the suspended candidate there

124

came unsummoned in./that portion of the vision/ the world applied to fill/ not unto nomination/ the cherubim reveal." He allowed us the time to grapple, first, with unfamiliar vocabulary; second, with the syntax needed to construct these ideas in free verse form; third, to come away with an interpretation that creative flashes of inspiration are heaven sent; and, fourth, provided the opportunity to evaluate that concept through the lens of our own perspectives. A lesser teacher would have taken the easy way here, providing an answer to a cohort that was itself ready for academic challenge, without such an aid, and thereby miss the chance to engage in authentic learning.

While it may be overstating the truth to credit my strong writing habits solely to Mr. Olio, his instruction certainly developed and reinforced my own ability to communicate my thoughts and insights clearly, in both formal and informal circumstances. Along with several other such excellent teachers, I would credit David with furthering my command of formal writing, in addition to other teachers at South Windsor High School. I came prepared in my undergraduate studies to engage in intellectual discourse, research papers, theses, and the like.

Additionally, in my freshman year [in college], David was among three teachers who allowed me to shadow them in their classrooms, as I attempted to discern whether or not I was called to be an educator (and, if so, in what capacity). Having only experienced an honors level course directly, I was impressed at how adeptly David adjusted his classroom procedures, rigor, and scaffolding to properly challenge students of all instructional levels. In doing so, David and his practice exercised Vygotsky's Proximal Zone of Development Stage Theory, etc. In short, David's educational approaches were tuned in each instance to whatever level was cognitively and developmentally appropriate for his students.

When word of this poem incident came out, I (as I'm sure many other former students of David) found it difficult to reconcile the level of scholarly acumen and erudite instruction found in his classroom. Piercing together details from various media outlets, I found myself searching the news on the Internet for David and stumbled upon several videos of his AP English classroom produced by the TeachingChannel.org (a resource for sharing professional development videos among teachers). For the duration of these videos, I truly found myself riveted not only from a sense of nostalgia but also at how seamlessly David incorporated today's technology into his instructional practices—which were remarkably tuned to the needs of the students, while also addressing the changing expectations laid out by the Common Core State Standards. Indeed David's classroom, as shown in these videos, is an environment perfectly balanced; not only do students think deeply, analyze text critically, and share ideas through writing and discussion effectively, they also demonstrate ownership over their learning via a classroom environment that affirms the place of each student's voice and ideas. For any who have never personally experienced being in his classroom, I can't urge you more emphatically to view these examples of a Master teacher at work.

Clearly his 22-year career as a teacher — 19 years of which have been served at South Windsor High School — are a credit to his legacy as a master teacher, and I hope my qualitative evidence likewise sheds light on the quality of scholarship and character this man has demonstrated in the vast majority of his time here. I, myself, would be shocked and quite honestly ashamed if this body were to proceed with terminating David's contract on the grounds of one incident. If nothing else, I call for a stay of any such action until the members of the Board of Education view examples of David's teaching available from the teaching channel website. There surely are other disciplinary measures available to deal with isolated incidents such as this. In light of David's record, which has been exemplary, and in light of his legacy as a master teacher at South Windsor High School for nearly two decades—and, particularly in comparison to other incidents where real tangible harm has fallen students as a result of willful and wanton disregard for their well-being health and safety by a teacher abusing his or her position or authority, I urge the board to carefully consider its options, which include unpaid leave in a time bound suspension and or public as well as private reprimands. In foregoing these options I fear the board is allowing the wildfire, emotionally charged outlet of social media to dictate policy, which diminishes actual constructive discourse to a mere shouting match and usurps the right of South Windsor community to exert its will through the duly elected officials; moreover, I feel that South Windsor Public Schools would become permeated by an environment and atmosphere of fear, in which teachers feel inhibited to say nothing. An unsupported administration will undermine authentically engaging students in the learning process. I fear for the deterioration of a school district so invested in the cognitive development and intellectual being of its students, and I fear that taking extreme disciplinary action in this instance will discourage talented educators from considering South Windsor as a place of occupation to the detriment of its future students.

Surely, a community which has thus far supported academic excellence and made by the board is fully informed and all matters regarding to Mr. David Olio.

This letter certainly speaks to treating students as highly capable learners, affording them the best opportunities to excel. More, it reminds us that writing helps carry the values important to us into the public square. Although his did not achieve its ends here, his entrance into the conversation matters most to me. Just incredible.

One of you, my sophomore students, also wrote me over and over to tell me that you knew I was not allowed to contact students. You kindly wrote, though, you were concerned for me. Broke my heart.

This student had been striving against difficult challenges at home. The silence the next day seemed to choke her, especially. This sharp, bright student had made incredible progress in American Literature, after having a difficult freshman year, missing a significant amount of school. As her sophomore teacher, I had worked with her special education caseworker to move her from my college preparatory level, American Literature section into my college preparatory Honors section. She demonstrated an amazing mind: sharp, insightful, mature. Her curiosity had not held her out of an honors placement in my estimation; rather, her infrequent attendance had. Not right in my mind.

I argued for her to move up a level, so she could engage with students who were more serious at that time in their lives: opening, questioning, probing. She blossomed in that Honors section. Her eyes pointed up more often, with chin pushing outwards—a pen twirled in her hand as she considered other's questions about Emily Dickinson's own retreat to her room, to write with insight. She began to give her thinking more voice, as she herself emerged from an academic cocoon. She offered a point about the contradiction of solitude and wondered about the role of writing. The paradox moved her. Her work was brilliant, connected, when called into the conversation. When she wrote asking how I was in this affair, I cried.

After, I could only contact her caseworker to tell her I was okay. That I would be okay. That everything would be okay. Our relationship prior had grown, for she said she felt visible, important in our classroom, after experiencing what she had called invisibility in her past. School had been hard for her. Isolating. Lonely. She had experienced the world beating down on her. Nevertheless, her empathy had poured out, so perhaps she could displace some pain in her life by looking to reach out and protect another. Her letters were willed with concern. Filled with balm. Filled with the lament of injustice. Unbelievable, really.

Even when sound is made in a vacuum, it quickly disappears, swallowed by the following silence. I guess I should not have been confused that the administration ultimately ignored the support voiced by so many. Voices of support for excellent teaching were swallowed by the administration's silence. You certainly couldn't know about all the letters written in support, because the South Windsor district administration and Board of Education never publicly released those documents, and the administration certainly did not respond to those who wrote, as far as I know. I do know the administration never engaged in a conversation surrounding the work of the classroom.

Unlike the "Irish Goodnight" where one ignores the disappears, I believe inquiry needs both interaction and oxygen to feed our waking lives. Silence, on the one hand, serves moments of quiet and meaningful reflection. It can afford time to tend to one's self. But intentional silencing of destroys. I'm trying in my letter to you to cast my own voice of advocacy amidst the silence surrounding that class to fill a void. The Gang. The others who wrote and spoke. Our work that school year, 2014-2015. All should not be left behind in silence. Poetry. Joy of discovery. Integrity Inquiry. Voice. Learning. Democracy.

10 YOU HAVE A DRAFT DUE TOMORROW

In 2003, just over 100 teachers gathered on a snowy Saturday at Trinity College in Hartford. The New England Association of Teachers of English (NEATE) had gathered Connecticut teachers—from kindergarten to college professors—to talk about writing. A group of students from SWHS walked up to the platform in the large hall to perform skits they had written as the introduction to the conference. As president, I introduced them, and then they acted out their first scene:

Setting: Two separate bedrooms, in separate houses. The night before a paper was due in English class. Seniors, they have notebooks in their laps on their beds. Each student holds a corded telephone. They just stare at their notebooks as they talk on the phone.

Ian

I have a draft due tomorrow. I don't know what to do.

Jan

What do ya mean?

Ian

What do you mean, 'What do you mean?' We have to bring a draft to class, so that we can share it, get feedback, and then revise it. Remember?

> Jan
> (eye-roll)

Tell me about it.

> Ian

Well, I'm thinking, wouldn't it just be easier to write the final draft first?

> Jan
> (intrigued)

Wha?

> Ian

You know, just write the final. Then dumb it down a bit after class. That way, I can turn in the all the drafts. Done.

End.

...

Gathered in a large hall, teachers burst into laughing. It's a challenge to design meaningful learning, and the students' skit dramatized that challenge. The teachers I learned from in my professional life somehow seemed to find the time and connect with other colleagues to develop their own professional capacity to support students with excellence. That's what professional people are driven to do. They seek out quality experiences to examine best practices. It's a habit of mind—an integrity of inquiry. They're always learning. As I write to you now, now that you are older, stepping into your own professional careers, you have your own working life squarely in front of you. You're likely thinking about not only the work itself but how you are going about it. You're thinking about the conditions of your work to help you grow and succeed. I imagine you're striving toward excellence in whatever line of work you're in.

Many of your teachers harnessed their own love of learning and made contributions to their profession to improve their practice for you. As president of NEATE from 2004 - 2006, I had proposed and organized the mini-conference for English professionals to talk about their reading and writing practices. The mini-conference, Conversations About Writing Across the Levels, which began with the hilarious skit, offered a unique design for conversation, creating time and space on a Saturday morning during the school year for teachers to share perspectives and learn about the needs of each other's students at unfamiliar levels. They had the opportunity to learn perspectives in curriculum design to meet those needs. Each participant there knew the stakes, for the No Child Left Behind Act of 2002 ushered in a new era of testing. Instead of focusing on rethinking and redesigning ways for teachers to engage with inquiries about improving their instruction and supporting striving student populations, more testing was added. I mean a lot more testing. So, teachers were especially concerned with the mandates they faced to prepare students for new state tests.

Well, for this mini-conference, we invited Peter Elbow, a writing professor at the University of Massachusetts, to be the key note speaker. A NEATE colleague on the Executive Board was connected to the Western Mass Writing Project, based in Amherst at UMass. A professor and writer who thought deeply about what it meant to guide and support students as writers, he advocated for teachers to make "lemonade out of lemons." Recognizing the national shift to do more testing to identify learning problems actually reduced teaching time, he advocated for teachers to spend time with students in conversation about their work—not simply to grade it. In short, "to assess," he said, draws from the French word "assier" which means to sit next to. And he advised that teachers continue their personal, important work with students; so, we can do this together, he said. We can "beat the bastards." Why spend inordinate time testing when we can spend time teaching. We can learn together. We can talk with students about their writing one-to-one, in small groups, and in large class conversations. Let's make this testing thing visible and work together through it.

I agree with Elbow. I also believe teachers and their teaching suffered under the accountability measure of test scores, that were not directly linked to their work. Inevitably, the focus shifted to "scores." It became quite evident in school districts' initiatives there was pressure to "improve test scores."

So, as I write you at this point of the letter, I share with you an underlying tension between the South Windsor Education Association and the district administration. Between teachers and administrators. Teachers felt ignored with administrators' seemingly endless calls for change without anything actually changing. Jumping through hoops missed the mark of learning. I was a teacher leader who called for teachers as autonomous learners, to focus on students. The work I did to support my profession and my colleagues did not, in my mind—and many other colleagues— sit well, to say the least, with our district administration.

To many, it was like going to work as a chef in a gourmet restaurant when the owner provides you fast-food ingredients and fryers. You know you can put together better recipes with better ingredients to suit the tastes of those dining, but you just aren't allowed to satisfy them. On top, in

2012, new national standards called Common Core State Standards—standards for your learning, were added to teachers' menus. What a crazy time teachers struggled to teach.

Let me tell you about a science teacher colleague at SWHS, though, who illustrates an individualized drive to be a better teacher. Great guy. Great model of a learner and teacher. I hadn't known this young teacher all that well, but we learned more about each other when he visited my classroom on his own one day, sitting in on one of my classes with my students. Just kind of showed up. He had heard his students talking up the book they were reading in my sophomore class. Ralph Ellison's *The Invisible Man*.

I can tell you the level of respect I have for this colleague, including his snarky irreverence. He not only gave up his own, personal time to read the book with students whom we shared, but he engaged in the highest level of scholarship by following his interest in ideas. He joined our conversation in a unit of inquiry titled, "Listening to Voices on the Lower Frequency." He jumped in. The man cares for ideas. He values students. Just great stuff.

We continued the conversation about teaching. We asked each other questions, probed strategies, and developed a great working relationship focusing on improving our work with students.

I'm sure you didn't know that a after semester of our collaboration, my colleague nominated me for an Excellence in Teaching award, given out by the Connecticut Education Association (CEA). He felt strongly about the work with diversity fairs, serving colleagues as president of NEATE, and pursuing student-centered teaching strategies with vigor. I was humbled. A bright, dedicated younger colleague, who

135

embodied a dedication to students and learning—a teaching professional, nominated me.

Well, I didn't win the award that year. "Better luck next year," he quipped. There are a lot of excellent educators, so it wasn't surprising; but, he and I continued to enjoy and learn from each other, talking about our students, our teaching, and their learning. I did win the next year when he nominated me a second time. (He wrote a better nominating letter.) That was 2009. I was awarded the Connecticut Education Association's Excellence in Teaching Award. Part of the award included a trip to Washington, DC, along with forty-nine other state winners sent to DC for a national award of Teaching Excellence. It was fabulous working with other colleagues in workshops that were part of the trip, listening to the incredible work teachers were designing and putting forward in their classrooms. We even had a session with Jane Goodall, who's work with teachers involved collaborating around issues of the environment and math and the sciences. I've had amazing colleagues at SWHS, across Connecticut, and across the nation.

When I returned, CEA invited me to chair the Commission on Instruction and Professional Development—a group of teacher volunteers dedicated to the study and sharing of teachers improving their practice. Did you know there even is such a thing? What a bunch of geeks teachers can be! We love teaching because we love learning. And we love you all, our students.

For the next five years I chaired the committee, working with twelve other appointees from throughout Connecticut to learn more about best practices of teaching by engaging in the study of professional development. The Commission sought to study best practices, share them, and empower teachers to improve their practice to serve their students even better.

I hope you're still with me during this part of my letter. I was working hard for teachers. For you. For learning. You're now at a point in your life you can put in context the behind-the-scenes conditions during our time together that would play a role in my severance. Teacher's work is generally on public display, but buried in the silence we find the limits placed on them in the current system. So, here I am, in front of you, on this page, sharing the story of hopes and challenges of professional collaboration.

I hope you're not hearing me say that teachers don't respect their administrative colleagues. That could not be farther from the truth. All my colleagues who have been to local, regional and national conferences or read journals from professional organizations know the value of other contributors to the conversation about excellence in teaching. To hear, know, and make one's own contribution to those ideas is a professional learner! So, please don't get me wrong.

When any working environment is built to include all voices, teachers, like students will give you every ounce of themselves. I say loudly, "Great collaborators make great teachers." By this point, my letter has asked a lot of you, bringing you into the world of teaching. I'm grateful for your audience, and I hope this exploration gives you a sense for the devotion teachers have for

The CEA asked me to serve as an appointee to the National Common Core Standards rollout conference, with other stakeholders from other state education associations, Denver, Colorado. To be transparent, CEA is an organization of unionized teachers. They provided me with lawyers to try to help defend against the legal action the district initiated. I'm grateful for the union's support for teachers in their practice against institutional injustice, despite that I ended up losing. I believe firmly in fully engaged teachers in local, state, and national conversations, but their inquiry and engagement need support by a reorganized system of equal footing for credentialed teachers. I agree the most important factor in a student's learning is a highly qualified teacher. I call for a system with teachers treated and working as professionals.

This is another loaded area of the conversation that you likely have heard in casual and perhaps even heated conversation: unions. I can only speak to my own experience and my own engagement. I know of multiple professional organizations designed to serve students and learning through the mine-field that is today's public-school teaching. While incredibly positive in my own growth as a teacher and educator, it also played a significant role in my being forced out from South Windsor. Unions have sought to defend teaching. I was an active member of our union, the South Windsor Education Association, and that put me into places of tension. As a union, we advocated for increased teacher participation in decision-making to improve their own practice.

You might be asking, why I write to you about the need for more teacher autonomy in my letter. This also sounds wonky, but it's more of the dark matter that never saw the light of day—and, I believe it played a role in the district's decision-making to force me out. Split open an apple and you'll find the seeds.

Tension bubbled between the administration and teachers after the change of a state law in 2014 sought to do this exact thing: give teachers a louder voice in their own professional development. It gave the teachers a binding vote in matters of how they learned to teach more effectively. The district, SWEA, and CEA, however, did not agree to an interpretation of the law. And the superintendent even called me in a meeting "a power grubber" to dismiss the new capacity. Yet the conditions were undeniable. The district yielded a slice of collaboration.

Indeed, I loved the inquiries into teaching strategies we engaged on the Commission on Instruction and Professional Development. It was exciting then to share that compelling research and discussion with colleagues. The CEA had designed a professional pathway to engage members of the union—the SWEA. Each district has a local, union branch of the CEA. They negotiate salaries and working conditions. They serve as an organized conduit for a large group of teachers. You may ask, why? Why do we have a system that necessitates a union? It's a good question.

I would love for there to be a better system, but the fact that public schools in the United States are funded by local taxes places teachers firmly under the public support system we now have. Teachers, firefighters, police, are all subject to the whims and necessities of budgets, and those budgets tend to struggle to provide living wages across the country. Public servants, like teachers, used to work two jobs when I began teaching, to make ends meet. My first teaching job in 1993 paid $19,000.

Moreover, tight budgets have prompted district practices to control, define, and determine working conditions, limiting the input from teachers and their own process of individual professional growth. Like the professions of medicine and the law, teaching needs educated, credentialed professionals to help make the best decisions. That's the notion of professionalism: learn, share, reflect, monitor, grow. Professionals collaborate and oversee each other. But unlike doctors and lawyers, in teaching, others control working conditions and credentialing.

To add to the tensions, the history of teaching salaries is dismal. Teachers across the country struggle with low pay and authoritative oversight. On top, todays' trends toward censorship and privatized religious schools receiving public funds further erodes public teachers' professional autonomy. Right now, I believe unions are the absolute best response to maintain public education for all citizens. Teachers absolutely need to create better learning conditions for ALL students, and they're being held back—and have been held back for years.

No one has talked about these issues to you in public, and we certainly have not discussed key changes to Connecticut law in 2012 as playing a role in districts sharing the responsibility of oversight. SWEA had appointed me to co-chair the newly created Teacher Evaluation and Professional Development Committee. which I did for about a year. Nothing but roadblocks. I remember my colleagues from SWEA—the president, vice president, secretary, and treasurer, attending a meeting with the South Windsor district administration, LED, of course, by the superintendent. We were negotiating after the passage of the new law. WE were supposed to engage in a new and more collaborative structure with the district to empower teachers to have a more directive role and set of responsibilities for themselves as practitioners. The change in laws and their requirements, held that teachers should have a binding voice in district teacher professional development. Instead, the meeting devolved into finger pointing, with the superintendent calling me that name: "a power grubber." Hmmm.

About a month before the reading of the poem, I resigned: at the end of January 2015. After multiple meetings and conversations with the administration, we could not agree on a more authentic collaborative process. I have always tried to bring my passion for the love of learning not just to my classroom but also to my profession—to my colleagues. To be involved with them. To learn with them. It just wasn't working.

I know. I hear you. This all gets very wonky. I understand. But you're now in your late twenties and these complexities have likely arisen in your own work in their own ways. Remember the questions I raised just a few pages ago? Re-read them, please. They're important for us. Trying to explain how the sausage is made stands another problem, though. It ain't simple. Life just isn't. The complexities behind the twelve minutes of a poem read by a major American poet and discussed by a second-semester senior AP/ECE class stand an example.

So, I write this letter about your former school district that lacked—in my experience—the embrace of teacher autonomy—of learning and collaboratively determining their own students' needs in order to meet them.

Professional development experts tell us as much. Teachers need to be empowered to be their best most authentic selves in their teaching, as educators. We need to accept and include all stakeholders in an authentic process, instead of simply being told what to do. So, the teacher evaluation changes in Connecticut State law further diminished teacher's ability to have a strong, binding voice in protecting themselves when they advocate and negotiate for their view of excellence in the classroom. Governor Malloy had been very upset about poor performance in Connecticut, especially with students with special needs. And in 2014, he oversaw another legislative change that significantly changed statutes to control teachers. The revised law removed two of the three arbitrators in an arbitration system designed to help settle disputes between districts and their teachers.

The change would seal my fate, as the Board of Education gained a final, binding say. With the tension still remaining, the superintendent would not relent and see fit to recommend to the Board my return to the classroom.

It's ironic: teachers are allegedly in control of writing lesson plans, designing unit plans, and structuring their classrooms and making decisions based on the students they have in front of them. Instead, people are not included, their motivation for inquiry diminishes, and so, too, opportunities for teacher's growth and improvement, to dance like waves of the sea.

It's tough out there, folks. Yet, teachers still have a draft of their lessons due tomorrow, and I'm confident they'll write them with the best they have.

11 BANNED

Because I've relied on the strength of words in this letter to reconnect with you and make visible and audible the complexities after our last day together in February of 2015, I'm especially distraught over the growing appetite to restrict, censor, and outright ban books.

The joy books bring unfortunately floats today atop an undercurrent of censorship in the United States.

The first time Allen Ginsberg's work caused a public stir was twenty-three years after James Joyce's *Ulysses* had been banned from coming into the United States. Joyce, as an artist, had turned away from traditional Irish narratives in the novel to examine the inward life of a middle-class Irishman over a twenty-four-hour period. Written with deep personal insight about human desire, culture, art, nationalism, and religion, the book was banned by United States government from import to the US in 1933.

In 1956, the publication of Allen Ginsberg's "Howl" put Lawrence Ferlinghetti, co-owner of City Lights book store, in jeopardy of jail for indecency for publishing the book of poetry. After the censorship case went up to California's Supreme Court in 1957 and was defeated, Ferlinghetti proclaimed in an essay, "Howl on Trial: The Battle for Free Expression," the ideas and language had already been "in the air, waiting to be captured in speech. The repressive, conformist, racist, homophobic world of the 1950's cried out for it." And, I'm not surprised but glad an intelligent California Judge, Hon. Clayton Horn, had the insight to recognize art—again—as an honest expression about our lives one way or another, up or down, left or right, inside outside. "Howl," he said was not obscene, but had redeeming social qualities. I think of art as a joyous and honest recognition of the human condition, including our human foibles. Judge Horn went on to write:

> The People state that it is not necessary to use such words and that others would be more palatable to good taste. The answer is that life is not encased in one formula whereby everyone acts the same or conforms to a particular pattern. No two persons think alike; we were all made from the same mold but in different patterns. Would there be any freedom of press or speech if one must reduce his vocabulary to vapid innocuous euphemism? An author should be real in treating his subject and be allowed to express his thoughts and ideas in his own words.

Wow. "An author should be real." In other words, the judge recognized the unreasonable urge to control and categorize language, rather than allowing language to describe humanity. Just as South Windsor Public School's response to the reading of Ginsberg in my class, the case against Ginsberg's poem in California centered on the use of words to suit people's tastes. After the reading, the local press would fall into line and continue the story as one of pending punishment for poor taste and a lack of judgment. Crews descended on the high school campus that following Monday morning. The report would air an interview with an anonymous parent who refused to be videotaped but would say that she "had no idea how the poem got into the classroom." The use of an anonymous parent as part of a news report was disturbing enough, but NBC CT news went on to interview a student, saying he was part of the class, when he was not. The student was presented as if he were in the class, which he was not. He would give an inaccurate account of the class. The news cycle then perpetuated the biased rumors of salacious sex that neatly fit into homophobic under currents.

The path of punishment began immediately. The beginning of my severance emerged during the first interrogation. My twenty-three-year career was reduced to a twenty-minute interview. I would explain to the assistant superintendent that I skimmed the poem before encouraging and leading our class to examine Steven's question about language. I thought it was teachable moment at the end of a class. Asked about the language, I replied that our course studied the relationship between form and content, and that the poem offered a compelling look at that relationship. I characterized the narrator's language as "harsh," and we were trying to unpack the narrator's construction. I shared my reading of the poem, of an ironic narrator, and the assistant superintendent said he didn't understand hidden meaning in poems.

He claimed the language was inappropriate, and I would be put on administrative leave. I was not to have any contact with any students, and I was not allowed back on campus or at any district of South Windsor event of any kind. The assistant superintendent and principal dispossessed me, as I've noted, of my classroom keys and my school ID badge. They reported the event to the police, who would later be quoted in a news report that the South Windsor Police Department would "not be investigating the matter." I was escorted from the building—and the district would see my encouragement of the poem through the lens of criminal abuse.

Security escorted me back to my classroom after the interview, so that I could gather my things. I was shaken and tried not to let a look of shock appear on my face as I entered the classroom with my Period 6 sophomore American Literature students watching me. Did not want them to be alarmed. We had worked together for six months, and the class had grown. They were concerned—you could see the confusion on their faces, as they peered up from their group work. They had been reading an article about the closing of the Hilltop Steak House in Boston, discussing the virtues and limits of a community losing an aged, iconic restaurant. A day before, my Department Chair had observed the class. He noted students were engaged and interested. Notebooks and the article they were reading lay open in front of them, pens were nervously twirled, and eyebrows were slanted upwards. I managed a half-smile and told them I needed to go, and that I would be thinking of them. It would be the last time I would see those of you in our Period 6 class—

...

The signs had already appeared in South Windsor. A year and a half prior to this cruelty, a parent challenged a summer reading book on the AP/ECE assignment, calling Haruki Murakami's novel *Kafka on the Shore* "pornographic." I learned of the challenge when I received notice from the department chair that the parent had challenged the book and demanded an explanation. I explained to my department chair the book selection process. My colleague, also teaching a section of the course, and I had selected the novel to fill a gap: we did not have any contemporary texts with males as narrators on the summer list. We had learned from students the year before they hoped for a more diverse list, that especially might appeal to young men— the list had featured such amazing books as the Victorian novel *Tess of the D'Urbervilles* and a mid-twentieth century memoir in *Warrior Woman*. So, we sought to include a contemporary and cultural male voice. Not only did Murakami's novel fit those criterion but also it offered a unique post-modern form, featuring two separate narratives woven together. The novelist would be considered multiple years for the Pulitzer prize. More, the juxtaposition would allow students' entrance into the pastiche world of literature that underscores so many narratives—and the beginning of the course.

However, during the conversation, the parent was firm that certain passages in the novel were pornographic and not fit for the "children" of South Windsor. The end result was that the book would be pulled and replaced with, ironically, *Catch-22*. I reported the incident to the American Library Association. Now, at this point, the parent had come in with the complaint, which was heard by teachers and administrators, and while I did not agree that the book should be pulled, at least there was a conversation. I am soundly in favor of students' freedom to choose what to read. If students didn't want to read *Kafka on the Shore*, they did not have to. The pressure was so great on the chair; it's difficult to say it was a stain on the English Department, but it clearly signaled an appetite to censor books in town by certain individuals. As I look back on February 26, 2015, the next day, it makes frightening sense that a union representative came to my classroom and excused me from the class in order for the assistant superintendent to take my room keys, my school badge, and put me on leave after twenty minutes in the main office conference room.

As I've pulled together the past for you, I would explain to him that I directed Steven to put the poem up and we'd discuss his question about language. Neither he nor the principal would acknowledge I was engaging a student's curiosity in a teaching moment. They were rooted in a set of assumptions that the language in the poem was not literary but "highly inappropriate." The superintendent would clearly judge the poem as "highly inappropriate" in a School Messenger notice to all parents in the district. The notice would go on to say that the district does not "tolerate" "highly inappropriate" language. In short, unlike the Supreme Court that would later affirm the California State Court, ruling in Roth v. The United States for freedom of speech against obscenity claims, the superintendent rejected any possibility of conversation about literature in an AP/ECE course.

At the risk of perpetuating a subtle and powerful message of homophobia that existed in the district—and still in many places in the country, a complex and complicated context of a literary discussions would instead be ignored in that School Messenger notice.

I'm saddened. We all know there be those who get a hold of my letter to you—this memoir—and say terrible things. That's a risk I take. For all attempts I've made in my drafts over the years, I have sought to negotiate the very problems that have slowed me in writing. My first draft, though, launched me into the unknown, and revision has brought waves of discovery. Writing has propelled me.

We live during a time of hotly articulated beliefs. We need ways to use words effectively to be open with each other. To be fair with each other. To strive toward inclusion, rather than exclusion. I hope that the assembly of some of these words gives you faith in our human ability to communicate in our relationships—and perhaps we can celebrate the positive effect our artistic shaping of words can have on our lives.

Still, as we pull material from the black hole, I raise a most central and most important topic in the conversation we've yet to have directly: the ongoing attacks and banning of ideas of inclusion and equity for the LGBTQ+ community. The words "inclusion" and "equity" have been glorified and celebrated. However, over the recent past some have sought to control and redefine them with aggressive language. Even legal attempts have been made to delegitimize a wide, beautiful swath of human beings for whom traditional binary definitions just do not fit. In fact, just prior to the publication of my letter to you, the federal government is conducting a full assault on the idea of equity and inclusion in 2025, with a ridiculous announcement that the federal government only recognizes a black and white binary gender definition. This denial of people's identity counters principles of human rights and democratic freedoms. At the epicenter of the response to Ginsberg's poem sits an uncomfortable truth: bias exists against people who identify in some way as on the LGBTQ+ spectrum. It pains me that students who had had an inkling they may identify as gay, lesbian, bisexual, trans, or questioning would hear these signals. I reject those signals, and I believe most people also reject them. May the words of my letter shout out for the humanity and capacity of each and every person.

I wondered how any LGBTQ+ student not only in my AP/ECE class but also in the school or any student who heard about this story on the local news—and what would become national news—would interpret these events following the fateful class. If my own sense of safety and identity, as teacher and educator, was so attacked, what about these young people? What about their sense of self? What about my colleagues? The school never said anything about this. The superintendent remained silent. So, I want to say here on this page in this book, ALL of you in my classes are respected, loved, and held as important people in our world. I say it OUT LOUD. I want to shout from the rooftop of the world that you are a joy in the world—and you are not alone!

I remember when we read The *Tragedy of King Lear*, a play that tests the limits of tragedy. Just how much pain can someone take in the world? Just how much should someone take? How far can art go to let us experience and understand those pains and consider the limits? I believe those who care about the world and are willing to suffer for that care are at the heart of the tragic spirit in *Lear*. Cordelia says in Act V, "We are not the first Who with best meaning have incurred the worst." I know our world seems unbearably ignorant at times toward people's humanity. You will encounter the ugliness that seemingly seeks to suffocate at some point. However, I'm convinced there are more ways to think about our responses and more new ways to value each person across our communities than there are slights against us.

We have people to comfort. I do believe that people are good: I have always embraced our capacity for good will. We need to have the courage to be ourselves and live out our understanding as best we can. We can use the language of empathy, as our conversations are difficult enough as it is.

Well, by now the extended metaphor of the black hole may have faltered, turning into a kind of mixed metaphor of sight and sound. That may mean our journey through words works in a way of disruption, sort of scattering not only the dense material before us but also my best intentions into unmanageable pieces. These words to you have sought out a conversation. I hope you hear me elevating the learning each of you deserve—that everyone deserves.

I had no experience in being banned. None. I've had disagreements. Yet, this experience as a public-school educator is entirely on another level. There was no training for such a thing. I had no idea what to do. My most private and public support has come from my partner, spouse, and best friend. When I first came home from school after that fateful class with my AP/ECE students, I told her about the most incredible experience that had crept up on me and my students in the last twelve minutes of class. I remember sitting in our living room with a neighbor-painter, who had finished the inside walls and trim of our house.

We had invited him over for a glass of wine and closing conversation to celebrate his work. I spoke of the class in short, excited breaths. The on-going interest of students in each other's work. The presentations. The poets' multiple perspectives and creatively artistic new forms. Then, the taking on of a very difficult poem. We discussed and prattled and wondered, amazed about the events of the day.

As the calendar read three days later, and I was told the district would move to terminate my contract, she stood shoulder to shoulder with me. As the slurs and threats came— and they came hot and heavy during those first weeks—she held my hand. She continued to gift me trust of heart. The public cruelty ran deep and ugly with claims of "crimes against students" that it felt as if a steamroller had caught us, first trapping our fingers, then pressing down on our knuckles, crushing our hands, and rolling toward the wrists... yet, she maintained her faith. When so many others seemed to have lost faith, my partner held me up. These words are written with emotion of gratefulness and love. I can only hope for you to have such a person in your life—one with an unconditional trust of goodness and acknowledgment of your joy in the world.

You've heard the phrase "unconditional love." It's a hell of a phrase. It's a real thing. It's a commitment to another's fundamental sense of dignity and humanity. It's a concept like a boat is tethered to a mooring. It holds and protects another's sense of stability. So when the district turned on me, leading and joining what felt like calls for my head, my best friend shouted her unconditional love.

I recall the day of the final interaction with South Windsor Public Schools. We met at a mutually agreed upon location to negotiate my return in Windsor, CT, or, at least that's what we expected. That's what my lawyers, who were provided by the CEA, had been told. We had all been sitting at a large oval table that included the superintendent, the board of education chair, and their lawyers from Shipman and Goodman that morning. We had split off into two separate groups, with an arbitrator meeting with each, bringing ideas back and forth. This went on for several hours in the morning. The length of time signaled a problem for me coming back.

I remember it to this day: the Board of Education Chair and I happened to be standing in the hallway during a break. He turned to me and flatly stated, "You'll never teach in front of my children." It was a shock to hear. It was a shock to also have heard the superintendent tell me earlier in our single, private meeting, "We live in a one-strike-and-you're-out world, so we have to get this behind us." So. It was over. Almost twenty years of work in the district that included an uncountable number of interactions with thousands of students and parents, like bringing a student's notebook and dropping it off to their house after school that they had forgotten, after a 7th Period class; like working with a parent to help bring in Jamaican food from her car during one of the diversity fairs; like designing and organizing field trips to the Mashantucket Pequot Indian museum and library in Montville, Connecticut.

I stepped outside after sharing the conversation with the CEA negotiating team, my hands shaking. I was short of breath. My wife had been traveling for business. She frequently took business trips to California and the West Coast, and this was a trip that she had had planned for a long time. We were in constant contact during the day. I called her again.

Ooohh, I remember the warmth and comfort of her voice. "Don't worry," she reassured me. "We'll get through this. Do the best you can."

"I love you, too." I hung up. When I returned just at noon to the table, literally and figuratively, the negotiations ended. The legal language of separation was then cobbled together: cold and formal contractual words. I thought, how can you put a price on learning? On a teaching career?

Well, it was written. I left.

When my wife returned from her West Coast trip, her words of love and comfort were enough. And they continue not only to be enough but also to nurture. As I write to you now, about having emerged from the storm, having shaken the rain from my shoulders, I confidently extend words of hope to each of you.

My wife and I worked together over the next weeks trying to figure to whom I could speak, whom I could contact, whom I could reach out to for help. And even under those circumstances, which threatened not just my livelihood but my sense of self as an educator, she locked arms with me. After, I kept reaching out, and the more I reached out the more support I received. Reaching out was just as awkward as it was trying to write a first draft to you. What do I say? How do I process and talk about all of this? A myriad of complex issues had formed a low ceiling of thick grey clouds, with a layer of fog, too, on the ground. I'm grateful for other's support. Here, I've been able to begin to piece together words of appreciation.

To contend with banishment is to open it up—and reach out of it. Writing has made this possible for me, in this circumstance, for this letter. Each draft teaches me more, and each has empowered new areas of exploration of writing itself. Here, I can recall the support from students, former students, colleagues, former colleagues, parents from town, and students from this class. I check back with the drawers full of words from former students who wrote me emails and letters. I remember walking to the mailbox early during early March 2015, to find beautiful handwritten letters. One student wrote to me that she was in Japan, and she just wanted to say that I had helped her during a very difficult time in her life, and that our class had supported her. She included in this handwritten note a Japanese good luck charm from a Shinto temple telling me that she hoped it would bring some comfort. Another student sent another good luck charm, this one Chinese. Both of these still hang from the cabinet handles in my kitchen as reminders of the classroom and my students. I received copies of letters written by my colleagues at SWHS, nearly 100 of them. It's important to be transparent: some of them disapproved of the poem itself being read in our classroom. I was able to speak with a few who felt reading the poem aloud was a mistake. I respect their perspectives.

Still, they supported me, the educator. They had known me for my almost twenty years of service. They had worked with me in one capacity or another, through committees or sharing a room for study hall. In fact, one colleague from the science department wrote a letter that was published in *The Hartford Courant*. In direct use of the honest language of a scientist, he felt it a terrible shame that the superintendent had not recognized my years of service; had not recognized my devotion to you all and to my other students; had not recognized my devotion to supporting South Windsor High School as a community of learners in so many ways. It was striking to me then, and as I write to you now, the language of a science teacher. He expressed clearly and firmly that he did not like the poem; in fact, he personally found it abhorrent. His response is an important one. He gave it voice just as I gave Ginsberg's work voice. He articulated his response in the highest order of intellectual, personal, and educational conversation. He entered the conversation about the expression of love for another man in a poem, and he was capable of separating his point of view from an educational experience of learning and teaching. His was an example of managing discretion. He managed the complexity, so I draw on his words of wisdom.

I admire the voices of students who wrote. I admire the voices of colleagues who wrote, and I admire those people who are strong enough and, moreover, compelled to enter into a public conversation about teaching and learning. So, I share these words with you to remind myself that things always don't go our way in the world. But if we remain open to discovering new paths, and we engage others in conversation, bringing our authentic and best selves, then that drive will turn into grace. To you, my former students, there have not been words more important to say to you. None of us are alone when in conversation.

. . .

And so I moved on. I joined the English Department at the University of Connecticut to continue the dance with students on the Hartford and Storrs campuses, ironically teaching in the same First-Year Writing Program that I had been teaching on the South Windsor campus. Imagine that.

For nearly seven years, I continued my own inquiry into course design and teaching that engaged students with the world through reading and writing. Commitment to scholarship and the needs of students drove a focus in the First-Year Writing program toward a place-based inquiry. Collaborating with colleagues to develop placed-based writing experiences taught me much about Hartford and Storrs. Mostly, our work taught me about the wide array of student experiences who come to the university from around the state and around the globe. We investigated the capacity for writing to propel us into important conversations to disrupt the common thinking. We need to get outside of our perspectives through research and reading to write the next chapter of the next generations lives. I hope you are remaking the places in which you live, into the places you want, hope for, and deserve.

These practices percolated in appointments at Springfield College, American International College, and Adelphi University. I found healthy places of learning again after leaving South Windsor Public Schools. I retired in late 2022 from the classroom after thirty years.

Dance. Reach out. Write a wrong, as my friend Kathy would say. I share with you in these last words of my letter the Allen Foundation: a non-profit born to offer words of comfort and support to those in the LGBTQ+ community, including their allies. I began this organization in 2019, after getting my feet back on the ground and restarting my work at the University of Connecticut in their First-Year Writing Program. It serves to raise awareness of the challenges that the community of students who are interested in LGBTQ+ issues and the arts face—to write wrongs. The foundation also serves as a fundraiser to offer scholarships to rising seniors in the Greater Hartford Area. Initially, I assembled an Executive Board comprising a student from the class, a former colleague from the South Windsor English Department, a parent of one of your classmates from AP/ECE, a librarian and media specialist from South Windsor, and a lawyer to help forge the project. We have held local speaking events at libraries in South Windsor and Rockville, created an online voice with a website that includes an application portal for those in search of scholarships and a Facebook page, and raised funds for scholarships, awarding our first scholarship in 2020. Portions of the proceeds from this book will go to the Allen Foundation. Please support this work in any way you can.

12 VALEDICTION

I'm so grateful for having the chance to speak to you again, and I'm blown away that I'm now writing these last words. Writing to you has been a gift. It has helped me build a voice out from beneath ten years of silence. (Can you believe it's been ten years? I can't!) Through revision after revision, I've discovered ways to collect experiences, press on them, and seek to use language to share them with you. The spirit has always been dancing inside me since we last spoke, so to finally find a way to place that spirit in front of you here makes me quiver.

If we are to imagine a place where we can actually talk to each other and thrive in new opportunities for work, play, and love, we'll need the confidence in the process of discovery. I believe that possibility inspires us, so if we share each other's imaginative thinking, we'll explode possibilities. Isn't that the stuff of democracy? Drawing from each other? Writing for me helps shape new thinking, and you and your generation have the tools for creative writing and thinking— together. You have the tools to bring about creative conversation.

I can't tell you how grateful I am for my 30-year joy fest of teaching. Having started teaching for three years at Cathedral High School in Springfield MA, to my 20 years at South Windsor High School, and closing with seven years teaching First-Year Writing courses at the University of Connecticut, I've played with millions of words. And during this exploration, I've grown: I've become a better father, husband, brother, friend, and person. I remember writing a letter to my former department chair at South Windsor after retiring from the classroom in December of 2022.

In that letter, I thanked her for her guidance and especially her passion for ideas, our students, and learning. The work we forged in the department in the '90s opened unfettered pathways to perspectives that I would have never imagined. It's the easiest part of this letter to write: I wish opportunities for each of you in your learning—to open and chase the world. I hope your learning never stops. May you remain aware in your experiences, my former students. May you have the tenacity of curiosity to open new doors of attention. I hope the same intensity and honesty is welcomed in your communities.

Of the over 2,000 students that I had the honor to work with at South Windsor, I've witnessed heroes: students and teaching colleagues. Heroes offer us hope for pathways of searching. In Joseph Conrad's observations of the archetypal journey of the hero, none of those qualities, as they unfurl, remain silent. None! No, they're shared through story. After all, the hero's journey is not just about success during the search but also the story of confidence in search itself.

Just as Steven, the young man who brought a book of poetry to class was inspired by other's conversation to search, we can learn about this crazy world found in experience, writing, song, and art. Steven remains an image of joyful pursuit.

As I write these last words to you, the value of the moment is at stake. I mean, the joy of being present in the moment relies on freedom to wander. To devote ourselves to an observation, we persist, like waves. The human spirit that feeds the search for our truths will not die; it will leap and bound. Let's invite idiosyncrasy, nuance, and difference into each moment of our day. Let's risk the search beyond the expectations of our everyday habits. That's an important step in growth, so with a confidence in inquiry we can strive. Allow yourself to read, write, and speak with others. Allow yourself to prompt others to ask you questions. Give yourself the grace to experience the freedom of thought to define dignity and truth for all people.

You have the power to create each moment. So after putting down this letter, may you take these words with you and make them you own. May you, too, dance like waves of the sea.

With admiration, a former English teacher of yours,

David

ABOUT THE AUTHOR

Over a thirty-year span of teaching English, David Olio, Jr. has been privileged to work with more than 3,000 students and hundreds of teachers in a variety of K-16 settings. He has worked as a classroom English teacher, a TESOL instructor, and Adjunct Professor of English. With degrees from St. Michael's College, Central Connecticut State University, and Trinity College, Hartford, he has shared his commitment to active learning that connects students to authentic learning beyond the classroom's walls. He's led professional development and curriculum development initiatives designed to support teacher growth and empower teachers as professional practitioners with the South Windsor Education Association, the Connecticut Education Association, and the University of Connecticut's First-Year Writing Program. He has presented his work over twenty times at local, state, and national conferences and events, and his work also appears on the *Teaching Channel*. He was the 2006 New England Association of Teachers of English's recipient of the Charles Swain Thomas Award: Contributions to the Profession; and, he was also the 2009 Connecticut Education Association's recipient of the John McCormack Award for Excellence in Teaching. David also founded and directs the Allen Foundation, a non-profit advocating for students interested in the arts and LGBTQ+ issues in Greater Hartford. Currently, David lives in Connecticut with Teresa, his spouse and partner of thirty-five years. He has two grown children doing amazing things with their lives. After retiring from the classroom in 2022, he has pursued his passion for just and equitable education as a writer in the educational technology world.